A NEW IRELAND

A NEW IRELAND

Memories and Reflections of Cardinal Cahal B. Daly

Edited by Gemma Loughran

VERITAS

Published 2023 by
Veritas Publications
7-8 Lower Abbey Street
Dublin 1, Ireland
publications@veritas.ie
www.veritas.ie

ISBN 978 1 80097 063 2

10 9 8 7 6 5 4 3 2 1

A catalogue record for this book is available from the British Library.

Designed by Jeannie Swan, Veritas Publications
Cover by Lir Mac Cárthaigh, Veritas Publications
Printed in Ireland by SPRINT-print Ltd, Dublin

Veritas Publications is a member of Publishing Ireland.

Veritas books are printed on paper made from the wood pulp of managed forests. For every tree felled, at least one tree is planted, thereby renewing natural resources.

CONTENTS

FOREWORD

Go the Extra Mile – Cahal B. Daly: Reflections on the Practice of Dialogue[1]

Cahal Daly was born in Loughguile in the beautiful Glens of Antrim on 1 October 1917, the third of seven children. His father, Charles Daly, was a primary school teacher, originally from Keadue, County Roscommon, and his mother, Susan Connolly, a trainee teacher at the time of her marriage, was a native of Antrim. Loughguile had a majority Catholic population and a significant Protestant minority. Relations between the two communities were characterised by good neighbourliness. In his book *Steps on my Pilgrim Journey*, Cardinal Daly recalls that several Protestant families had sons studying for the ministry as he as studying for the priesthood. Anticipating his later commitment to ecumenism, Daly formed friendships with many of these, 'friendships which were maintained throughout later life and were greatly cherished'.[2]

1 This text is adapted from a lecture by Archbishop Paul Richard Gallagher marking the centenary of the birth of Cardinal Cahal Daly, which was given in Queen's University, Belfast, on 6 October 2017 and published in the form of a pamphlet by Shanway Press. Reproduced with the kind permission of Archbishop Paul Richard Gallagher and Shanway Press.

2 Cahal B. Daly, *Steps on my Pilgrim Journey: Memories and Reflections*, Dublin: Veritas, 1998, p. 16.

Educated at St Patrick's National School in Loughguile and subsequently in St Malachy's College, Belfast, Cahal Daly entered the seminary and studied classics at Queen's University, obtaining his BA with honours and the Henry Medal in Latin studies in 1937 and completing his MA the following year. The professor of Latin, Robert Mitchell Henry, took a keen interest in this promising young student and encouraged him to study for a master's degree, and take as his topic 'The Church in North Africa in the time of Tertullian'. This prompted a lifelong interest in the Fathers, which would eventually lead to a doctorate in theology and friendship with such outstanding representatives of the twentieth-century renewal of Catholic theology as the French Jesuit theologian Henri de Lubac.

Cahal Daly completed his studies for the priesthood at St Patrick's College, Maynooth, where he was ordained on 22 June 1941. Before leaving Maynooth, under the influence of two professors, Dr Peter McKevitt and Dr Cornelius Lucey, later bishop of Cork and Ross, Cahal Daly and his fellow ordinands took the momentous decision to found a society of priests, which was soon given the name 'Christus Rex' and whose aims included the promotion of the Church's social teaching and assistance to priests in all forms of work for social justice. Daly was to chair the Christus Rex Society for twenty-five years up to his retirement from the office in 1966. By bringing social teaching into the mainstream of the Church's life, the Society played an important role in the renewal of the Catholic Church in Ireland in the years leading up to the Second Vatican Council and in its immediate aftermath. Later, as a bishop, especially in the diocese of Down and Connor, Cahal Daly would give considerable attention to social problems, not hesitating to speak out against complacent economic policies which failed to acknowledge what he termed 'the correlation of violence with deprivation', referring to the phenomenon of violence in urban areas of high unemployment and rural areas of struggling small farms.

In 1945 Cahal Daly was appointed lecturer in scholastic philosophy at Queen's University. Some years later, in the academic year 1952/3, Queen's granted him sabbatical leave, which he spent studying at the Catholic Institute in Paris, where he obtained a licentiate in philosophy. Contact with the main currents of contemporary French philosophical thought and with the multi-faceted Catholic revival then taking place in France, particularly in the areas of theology, liturgical renewal, pastoral innovation and evangelisation, was to make a lasting impression on the young university lecturer, preparing him for the role he would later play as theological advisor to Bishop William Philbin and to the future Cardinal William Conway at the Second Vatican Council. Referring in retrospect to his French experience, Cahal Daly says:

> France has been a source of inspiration for me in my life as priest and as bishop. The experience was an excellent preparation for the Vatican Council when it came. More immediately, it transformed – or so I hope – my whole approach to the teaching of philosophy. In the early years of my teaching it was not always easy to get students to ask themselves the questions which serious philosophers ask. In my first years of teaching philosophy we still lived in a society where custom and tradition were highly valued and where radical questioning was rarely encountered. It

> was an age which, broadly speaking, expected things to remain more or less the same as they had been and which did not anticipate radical change in society or in the Church. In university teaching the traditional type of didactic lecture still prevailed and dialogue between professor and student was not yet common.[3]

During the 1960s, various factors contributed to a change in this regard, including universal free secondary education, greater opportunities for third-level education, new industrial developments and the advent of television. As Cahal Daly puts it, 'Ireland began to share the new mood of questioning of what had been and of greater confidence in what could be. We began to move from a society based largely on stability to a society more oriented towards change.'[4]

Welcoming the challenges posed by these developments, Cahal Daly sought to apply fresh methods to the teaching of philosophy, taking into account the new questioning mood of the young. He saw this not as a threat to be faced down in authoritarian fashion but as a welcome challenge to complacency, to be met with a listening heart and in a spirit of dialogue, in the conviction that ultimately Christ is the answer to the deepest questions of humankind.

Cahal Daly's background as a university lecturer and his later experiences in France and at the Second Vatican Council served as a preparation to take on the pastoral challenges of a rapidly changing society when he was appointed bishop of Ardagh and Clonmacnois in 1967. Fifteen years later he was transferred to his home diocese of Down and Connor, which at the time was going through the trauma of 'the

3 Ibid., p. 111.
4 Ibid., p. 112.

Troubles'. Following the unexpected death of the well-loved Cardinal Tomás Ó Fiaich, Cahal Daly was appointed archbishop of Armagh in 1990, at the age of seventy-three, and in the following year was made a cardinal by Pope John Paul II. Retiring in 1996, he dedicated his remaining years to prayer, study and writing. He died on 31 December 2009, at the age of ninety-two, a few days after the tragic fire which engulfed St Mel's Cathedral in Longford, where he had been consecrated a bishop forty-two years before.

Cahal Daly's episcopate was very much shaped by the teaching of the Second Vatican Council, which he attended as a theological expert. Neither an 'intransigent' nor a 'progressive', he admired the patient approach of Pope Paul VI aimed at obtaining general consensus, while demonstrating strong sympathy with bishops and theologians who insisted on the need for renewal and reform. The Council documents, which Bishop Daly frequently quoted in his speeches and writings, guided his cautious approach to the implementation of numerous post-conciliar pastoral, liturgical and catechetical reforms. Well aware of the various conflicting interpretations of the Council, he insisted on fidelity to the text and the necessity of balance:

> Perhaps the diversity of interpretations of the Council is related to the point of view from which one approaches it. Some seem to begin with *Gaudium et spes*, on the Church in the Modern World, and give priority to the world, to which the Church has to be related. Perhaps they need to rediscover that the Church which has to relate to this world is the Church whose first duty is to worship God and seek his face (*Sacrosanctum Concilium*), the Church of *Lumen*

> *Gentium*, the Church whose mission is to proclaim God's word to the world (*Dei verbum*). Correlatively, then, critics, of today's 'progressives' need to resist any temptation to retreat into what Congar called 'world-less' spirituality and sanctuary-bound and sacristy-confined clericalism. The true message of Vatican II rejects both extremes.[5]

In the Irish context, Cahal Daly's episcopate also required particular attention to ecumenism, to the promotion of peace and reconciliation during the troubled years of the Northern Ireland conflict and, especially in the latter years, to the shifting patterns in Church–State relations arising from social, cultural and political changes. In *Steps on my Pilgrim Journey*, Cardinal Daly does not hesitate to speak also of the 'dark shadows' in his life as bishop, caused by personal bereavement, continued violence in Northern Ireland and scandals in the Church, in particular the sexual abuse of minors perpetrated by priests and religious. While recognising that this crime is not confined to any particular group in society, he acknowledged that it is particularly heinous when committed by a priest or religious because of 'the added outrage of the violation of a sacred trust and a despicable abuse of the friendship, confidence and respect, or sometimes even veneration, in which the priest or religious was held by the family and by the child'.[6] During the final period of his episcopal ministry in Armagh, the Irish Bishops' Conference developed its first responses to this tragic reality.

Despite the 'dark shadows' and the difficulties which the Church in Ireland has had to face in recent years, Cardinal

5 Ibid., pp. 161–2.
6 Ibid., p. 274.

Daly never surrendered to despondency but, as a man of faith, concludes his reflections on a positive, hope-filled note:

> This is emphatically not a time for discouragement at how little we have done or for mere remorse for what we have failed to do. It is not a time for pessimism or fear about the future. The Holy Spirit has worked powerfully in the Church in our time, and continues to work mightily among the priests and lay persons who constitute the People of God. The fruits of the Second Vatican Council are only now beginning to mature. The fields are only ripening for harvest. The seeds of the Kingdom grow slowly, but they grow by their own God-given innate power 'even when we sleep'.[7]

Given Cahal Daly's convictions and experiences it is not surprising that he is especially remembered as a man of dialogue. In fact, dialogue provides an interpretative key to his pastoral approach and to his commitment to ecumenism, the Northern Ireland peace process and the development of Church–State relations. Even a cursory reading of the late Cardinal's writings and speeches shows clearly that his commitment was not prompted simply by pragmatic concerns, as though dialogue were merely a tactic to attain one's ends. Instead, he saw dialogue as having a solid theological foundation, giving rise to a moral obligation.

In this, Cahal Daly was deeply influenced by the first encyclical of Pope Paul VI, *Ecclesiam Suam*, which he describes as 'a masterly study of the nature of dialogue, the spirit and attitudes which it requires, the methodology it

7 Ibid., p. 518.

should follow'.[8] This document was published in 1964 while the Second Vatican Council was still in full swing. While not intending to decide the various questions which the Council Fathers were then debating, the Pope wished to provide some guidance on how the Church should understand and carry out her task today. The encyclical is divided into three parts. The first two are concerned with the need to see the Church as mystery, deepen awareness of her mission and identify the principles to ensure authentic renewal. The third part, which is directly related to our theme, is devoted to dialogue.

Pope Paul insists that the origins of dialogue are transcendent; it is rooted in God's intention to engage in a dialogue of salvation with humankind. This dialogue is motivated by love; it has no limits; it is without calculation; it does not impose or coerce, but respects freedom; it is not discriminatory, but universal; and it requires patience because it can be slow. The Church's relations with the world should adopt the form of dialogue on the model of the divine dialogue of salvation. In this context, dialogue is a way of exercising the apostolic mission; it is an art of spiritual communication, marked by clarity, meekness, trust and prudence. Dialogue involves presenting the fullness of the truth in a manner accessible and attractive to others and in a climate of friendship and service. Cahal Daly was particularly struck by Pope Paul's insistence on 'how we must approach those with whom we enter into dialogue, with love for their person, with respect for their sincerity, listening and not just refuting, persuading and not dismissing'.[9] In short, as he puts it, 'the Church's dialogue must always be a dialogue of love'.[10]

---

8 Ibid., p. 180.

9 Ibid., p. 410.

10 Ibid., p. 411.

With whom should the Church and her members engage? Pope Paul says that no one can be excluded, since the Church has a message for all. In this context, he speaks of the concentric circles of those with whom we should engage: with every human person, with those who believe in the divine, with other Christian brothers and sisters, and within the Catholic fold. Referring to ecumenical dialogue, the Pope recognises the difficulties posed by the Petrine office and emphasises that it must be understood as a primacy of service, ministry and love. Dialogue within the Catholic Church must be characterised by charity, obedience and authority exercised as service and as a ministry of truth and charity.

Ecclesiam Suam would profoundly shape Cahal Daly's commitment and approach to dialogue. Indeed, following Pope Paul's model of concentric circles, he sought to promote dialogue with all who were prepared to engage with him, especially within the local Church; with the leaders of the other Christian Churches in Ireland; with those involved in efforts to overcome violence in Northern Ireland and with political leaders, both North and South. He was particularly aware of the pressing need to dialogue with those who, for various reasons, have distanced themselves from the Church, as he explained in a most striking way in his installation homily in St Patrick's Cathedral, Armagh, on 16 December 1990:

> There are people and there are groups who feel estranged and alienated from the Church and who do not experience the Church as interested in them or as listening to them. A bishop, as a pastor who should take the Good Shepherd as his model, must go out to them too, he must offer dialogue to them

> too. There is no real dialogue without listening; and therefore the bishop must be a good listener. He must be open to learning from these people and to receiving from them, knowing always that Christ, in whose name he acts, and only Christ, knows and can judge the secrets of the heart, and knowing that, if he, the bishop, listens, Christ will hear and Christ will act through him and will speak the word which stills the storm and bids the angry waves be still.[11]

As a pastor who strove to implement the reforms of the Second Vatican Council regarding the exercise of the episcopal office, Cahal Daly identified collaborative ministry and dialogue as one of the priorities of the bishop's ministry. The Council's decree *Christus Dominus,* on the bishop's pastoral ministry, enjoins the diocesan bishop to consult with his priests individually and collectively, on a regular basis, especially about pastoral matters. Referring to this exhortation at a meeting he held with the priests of the diocese of Down and Connor shortly after his transfer to that diocese in 1982, Bishop Daly asked his priests to assist him in making this a reality:

> For myself, I wish, not just to talk, but also to listen; and there is no use in my listening if I am not to be told the truth, or if I am to be told only the things I like to hear, the things that perhaps flatter me and persuade me that all is well. The work that you and I are put here by the Lord to do is far too serious and far too urgent for that kind of nonsense. It is just

11 Ibid., p. 410.

> waste of time, waste of the Lord's time, the time he gave us to work for his Kingdom. A bishop is called to be a friend to his priests. If a person is to be your friend only when you flatter him, then his friendship is doing no good either to you or to him. We can do Christ's work only when we are together seeking the truth.[12]

While he strove to exercise his responsibilities in a collaborative way and was not slow to encourage priests and express his gratitude to them for their generosity and fidelity, particularly in difficult circumstances, Cahal Daly was also prepared to admit his mistakes and ask forgiveness, as he did in exemplary fashion on taking his leave of the priests of Armagh in 1996.

Cahal Daly also sought to encourage team ministry among priests and lay involvement and partnership at diocesan and parochial level, in accordance with the Council's vision of the Church. He was well aware that team ministry, even among priests who have excellent personal relations, does not come easy:

> It has to be patiently and perseveringly worked at. It calls for deliberate effort and planning. It requires regular dialogue and reflection on the problems and the opportunities, the needs and the resources of the parish. It needs to be regularly reviewed; a sense of mutual accountability within the team needs to be developed. Above all, team ministry requires commitment to community prayer on the part of the priests involved.[13]

---

12 Ibid., pp. 327–8.

13 Ibid., pp. 511–12.

Cahal Daly insisted that collaborative ministry should also include lay parishioners, since he was convinced that when laity are involved, 'team ministry takes on new significance and new power to revitalise a parish'.[14] He made it a rule that at least half of all members of parish pastoral councils, the diocesan pastoral council and diocesan commissions open to lay people should be women. He was particularly attentive to the spiritual and theological preparation of the members of these bodies, since he was convinced that without an adequate understanding of the Church and her mission and of the respective and complementary vocations of priesthood and laity, lay people would not be properly equipped to place their spiritual and human gifts at the service of the Church, side by side with priests and religious. With good preparation, lay people would not pose a threat to priests but would prove a great support to them. By taking on organisational and administrative tasks, they would enable priests to concentrate on their fundamental duties as evangelisers, teachers of the faith, leaders in prayer, spiritual directors and builders of communities of faith. At the same time, by working in a spirit of dialogue and partnership, priests and laity could grow together in faith and love, contribute to the growth of the Church as communion and witness together to the mystery of God and his love before the world.

Given his lifelong friendships with Christians of other denominations and the particular circumstances of Northern Ireland which lent particular urgency to the task, Cahal Daly was deeply convinced of the necessity of ecumenical dialogue:

---

14 Ibid., p. 512.

> The growth in unity within the Church must motivate us also to pray and work for unity between the Churches. Ecumenism is not an optional extra for priests or for laity. It is a command of the Lord and a response to his own prayer. The ministry of reconciliation which bishops and priests have received from the Lord through the Apostles is incomplete unless we are working also for reconciliation between divided Christians.[15]

From the outset Cahal Daly was involved with the Ballymascanlon Inter-Church meetings and succeeded in establishing excellent relations with leaders of the other Churches. He was well aware of the difficulties, ranging from hostility, suspicion or indifference to foolish enthusiasm and naïve optimism, but this did not deter him from continuing to work loyally and lovingly for ecumenism, in fidelity to the directives of the Second Vatican Council. Taking his cue from Paul VI, he insisted on the primacy of spiritual ecumenism, by which he meant a change of heart and holiness of life, rooted in prayer. All bitterness and bigotry should be purged, while attitudes of mutual understanding, mutual respect and the presumption of reciprocal good faith, sincerity and integrity should be cultivated. Charity, Daly believed, is the soul of dialogue:

> We must cultivate, in the words of Father Congar, 'an a priori of love and trust'. We must be eager to learn from one another, to receive from one another, rather than to discredit or triumph over one another. We

15 Ibid., p. 513; see also Cahal B. Daly, 'Ecumenism in Ireland Now: Problems and Hopes', *Irish Theological Quarterly*, Vol. 45, No. 1 (1978), pp. 3–27.

> must, once and for all, renounce any idea that one of us could succeed through the other's failure, could prosper in the other's adversity, or rejoice in the other's loss. Catholics must learn to rejoice in the Christian faith and fervour and witness of Protestants, and Protestants must learn to rejoice in those of Catholics. We must see ourselves as struggling together and trying to support one another in the struggle to be faithful in witnessing to the same Lord amid the testing of the faith which marks our times.[16]

During Cahal Daly's episcopate, much progress was made in ecumenical dialogue in Ireland, although he was also aware of the danger that it could be limited to small groups of specialists, with little impact on the lives of the individual faithful. He encouraged greater knowledge and study of the documents produced by various ecumenical discussions and recommended that the principles of ecumenism and some initiation into its practice should be regarded as indispensable elements in all religious education programmes, so that the fruits of ecumenical dialogue could percolate to all levels of the Church, thus facilitating mutual understanding and reconciliation between divided Christians. Although he was a staunch defender of Catholic schools and attracted criticism in certain quarters for his unwillingness to promote integrated education, Daly insisted on the need to promote the ecumenical spirit in the formation of Catholic pupils at all levels.

Cahal Daly's unwavering commitment to ecumenism was deeply rooted in his love for Christ and his desire to have 'the same mind as was in Christ Jesus'. As he put it,

16 Daly, 'Ecumenism in Ireland Now', p. 13.

> It is Christ who is the source of ecumenical conviction, the ground of ecumenical hope and the goal of ecumenical striving. He is the Alpha and the Omega of ecumenism. It is He who calls us to oneness in Himself. He is our oneness already realised. As we in our different Communions and in converging dialogue draw into closer communion with Him, we also by that very fact draw closer in communion with one another in Him. The exercise may be long and the effort painful. It was when He would be 'lifted up', Christ promised, that He would 'draw all things to Himself'. The 'lifting up' was by ropes and nails to a cross before it was elevation in glory. Christ's 'lifting up' was long and slow and painful. Can we expect it to be different for us, before we attain 'unity in our faith and in our knowledge of the Son of God, until we become the perfect Man, fully mature with the fullness of God Himself'?[17]

Although the pursuit of Christian unity through dialogue is a distinct undertaking from the quest for peace, ecumenical dialogue assumed particular urgency during the years of the Northern Ireland conflict. The leaders of all the major Christian denominations made strenuous efforts to bring an end to the violence which caused untold suffering to people on all sides of the religious and political divide.

As bishop of Down and Connor and later as archbishop of Armagh, Cahal Daly made an important contribution to the peace process. Apart from his strong and unambiguous condemnation of violence, no matter where it originated, and

17 Ibid., pp. 25–6.

his encouragement to those involved to engage in dialogue, he made valiant efforts to convince the civil authorities to deal with the excesses of the security forces, guarantee humane conditions for prisoners and tackle the social injustices and deprivation which fuelled resentment and provided a breeding ground for paramilitary involvement.

One of Cahal Daly's most important and courageous contributions to the peace process was his insistence on the need to recognise and respect the two traditions, Unionist and Nationalist, in Northern Ireland and their respective civil and political rights and aspirations. Without this, he was convinced, there could no political solution and no peace in the North. In the volume *The Price of Peace*, published in 1991, he explained it thus:

> Northern Ireland's problem is that of how to find ways of sharing two traditions, not ways of suppressing one or other tradition, or of subordinating one to the other. It is a problem of giving political expression to two equally valid loyalties, which each have an equally valid historic and moral right to be, and to be constitutionally recognised as being, an integral part of Northern Ireland. Recognition of two Ulster loyalties, two Ulster identities, is an indispensable precondition of any solution to the complex problems of Northern Ireland.[18]

Given this situation, Cahal Daly was convinced that the two communities would have to 'find ways of coexisting in peace and equality with one another, without either community

18 Cahal B. Daly, *The Price of Peace*, Belfast: The Blackstaff Press, 1991, pp. 5–6.

demanding of the other that it abnegate its sense of nationhood or renege its political convictions'.[19] This naturally would call for dialogue, as Daly stated in characteristically strong terms:

> Words of peace and reconciliation are words of life. Words of bitterness and violence are words of death. They conceal a death wish, or they contain an implicit and symbolic murder wish. Those who refuse to dialogue with others, who will not accept the right of others to be different, who will trust or will share with only those 'of our own kind', are secretly wishing that the others were not there, were not alive; they are implicitly willing their death.[20]

Despite the seemingly insurmountable obstacles to finding an acceptable political solution, Cahal Daly never became despondent, convinced as he was that Christianity would have the last word, and that word is love. Because of Christ, he said, 'we cannot despair of peace with justice, reconciliation, forgiveness and love in Ireland', for to despair of that would be to despair of God himself.[21] Faith has its imperatives, also in the political realm. As Cahal Daly put it:

> To believe in God's love towards ourselves is to believe also in God's love towards others, even when they are different from ourselves. It is to believe in the rights of others to be different from ourselves. The wish to extinguish differences is secretly a wish to eliminate those who dare to differ. Reconciliation

19 Ibid., p. 14.
20 Ibid., pp. 14–15.
21 Ibid., p. 15.

> across accepted differences is a direct consequence of believing in 'God's love towards ourselves'.[22]

As the peace process gathered momentum during the 1990s, Cahal Daly redoubled his efforts to persuade all involved to grasp the opportunity, abandon violence and embrace the cause of love, justice, peace and reconciliation. He was convinced that in the long term, 'the constitutional position of Northern Ireland [would] be determined by the evolution of the political process between its two communities and by democratic dialogue between its two traditions'.[23] No solution could be imposed from outside; only a change of heart on all sides could bring about an acceptable political solution.

Notwithstanding some setbacks on the way, the courage and commitment of Northern Irish political leaders on all sides, assisted and encouraged by the American, British and Irish governments, eventually led to the Good Friday Agreement of 1998. The principle of constitutional recognition of the legitimate civil and political rights and aspirations of the two traditions in Northern Ireland, on which Cardinal Daly had insisted, would prove fundamental to the power-sharing institutions which the Agreement established.

By then in retirement, Cardinal Daly warmly welcomed the Good Friday Agreement and prayed for its success, mindful as he was of the need for continued restraint and responsibility on the part of all concerned. No doubt, he would remind us today of the need to continue to engage in dialogue and go the extra mile in order to overcome the

22 Ibid., p. 15.
23 Ibid., p. 36.

difficulties that crop up from time to time. As he wrote some years earlier, 'there is no alternative to dialogue'.[24]

Cahal Daly's approach to the question of relations between Church and State in today's Ireland is also influenced by the same commitment. He was well aware of the frequent calls for 'separation of Church and State' and of the misunderstandings that arise in connection with this notion. In fact, there is no single universal model of separation, as the political systems of various countries clearly demonstrate. Cahal Daly certainly believed that Church and State should be seen as distinct and autonomous in their respective realms. As he stated at the New Ireland Forum in 1984, he was not favourable to the concept of a confessional State, since such an alliance between Church and State would be harmful to both. At the same time, he did not believe that the Church should remain silent on all matters of legislation and social concern, as though she had no right to take public positions and issue moral judgements on social and economic questions. To impose silence in these matters would be a denial of the fundamental democratic principle of religious liberty, which requires that the Churches have full freedom to proclaim the gospel. There obviously can be laws which are in conflict with the moral teachings of the gospel and the Church must have the freedom to point this out. While the Church does not expect civil legislation to conform to Church teaching, it does have 'the right and duty to form and to inform the consciences of those citizens who are Catholics about the moral implications and the moral consequences of proposed laws or constitutional changes, leaving it to their duly informed consciences how to act and how to vote'.[25]

24 Ibid., p. 185.

25 Daly, *Steps on my Pilgrim Journey*, p. 486.

Separation of Church and State 'cannot entail separation of either legislator or voter from his or her conscience'.[26]

In other words, while recognising that there are other legitimate considerations to be taken into account in drafting legislation, the Church claims the right to contribute to the debates about the formulation of laws and, more generally, about issues affecting the lives of citizens. The Church's contributions are not matters of faith only; 'they are also open to reasoned conviction on the part of any citizen, and they are often accepted by people of different traditions on grounds of reason, rather than on grounds of faith.'[27] Obviously, if something is good and true in itself, it does not cease to be so because the Catholic Church teaches it!

Naturally, the Church seeks to engage in public debates and put forward her position in a spirit of dialogue and respect for the institutions of the State and the democratic right of citizens to express themselves. Tensions, disagreements and even divisions can arise, but this is part of any normal healthy democratic process. Mature relations between Church and State are characterised neither by subservience nor by opposition but by what the Second Vatican Council calls 'wholesome, mutual cooperation' (cf. *Gaudium et spes*, 76) with due respect for the legitimate autonomy of both sides.

Although Cardinal Cahal Daly died before the election of Pope Francis, there are some interesting points of contact between them. The recent Jubilee of Mercy served, among other things, to raise awareness about the plight of prisoners; indeed visiting prisoners is one of the seven corporal works of mercy. Like Pope Francis, Cardinal Daly devoted considerable attention to the pastoral care, humane treatment

26 Ibid., p. 487.
27 Ibid.

and rehabilitation of prisoners, insisting on the need for mercy and clemency in their regard. Mercy and clemency, he maintained, are not only Christian virtues; they can also be 'forces for political change and social transformation'.[28] A further similarity lies in the Cardinal's emphasis on dialogue, which shows him to have been a promoter of what the Holy Father calls a 'culture of encounter'. The Pope uses this expression to emphasise the need to step out of our own comfort zones, to be fearless in looking beyond our own needs and aspirations to those of others and to go out and meet them. This is how encounter takes place.

Like dialogue, the culture of encounter is not a mere technique for ensuring better human relations but is theologically rooted in our prior encounter in faith with the love of Jesus. Jesus takes the initiative in encountering us and prompts us to do as he did: encounter others. Encounter overcomes isolation and exclusion; it implies respect for the dignity of others and seeks to establish interpersonal relations with them based on mutual respect, love and reciprocity. It implies risk, because in reaching out to others we expose ourselves and become somewhat vulnerable. This is because authentic encounter requires a response: we reach out to others in the hope that they will not reject our overtures but will grasp the opportunity to engage with us. We could make mistakes but this should not deter us. As Pope Francis once said: 'What happens if we step outside ourselves? The same as can happen to anyone who comes out of the house and onto the street: an accident. But I tell you, I far prefer a Church that has had a few accidents to a Church that has fallen sick from being closed.'[29]

---

28 Daly, *The Price of Peace*, p. 109.

29 Pope Francis, Address at the Vigil of Pentecost with the Ecclesial Movements, 18 May 2013.

Building a culture of dialogue naturally involves risks and possibilities, similar to those mentioned by Pope Francis when he speaks of a Church which is willing to step outside herself. Dialogue is obviously challenging and difficult. It requires much patience and perseverance. It requires us to face up to those forces of prejudice and entrenched positions within our own communities and indeed in our own hearts which hinder the possibility of accepting others as they are and listening to their legitimate concerns and aspirations. Despite the possibility of failure, we must never give up trying nor should we surrender to pessimism and despair. The only alternative is the imposition of the logic of power, whose tragic consequences all over the world are plain for all to see. Hence, there is a moral imperative to pursue dialogue. We must do so in season and out of season, honestly and transparently, with a listening ear and an open heart.

Cardinal Cahal Daly was an impressive Irishman and an outstanding son of the Church. His teaching on dialogue has lost nothing of its relevance and urgency. Let us learn from his example and act always in accordance with the spirit of dialogue which he sought to inculcate and promote. Above all, no matter what it may cost, let us be courageous and never hesitate to go the extra mile.

Archbishop Paul Richard Gallagher
Secretary (relations with states) of the
Holy See's Secretariat of State

PREFACE

It was both a privilege and a challenge to receive the invitation from Veritas to edit some material from the writings and addresses of Cahal Brendan Daly for publication to coincide with the twenty-fifth anniversary of the Good Friday Agreement.

The privilege has been involvement in a project that in some way marked the contribution to life in Ireland, both north and south, of a truly inspirational and wise pastor. The challenge has been in making the selection from Cahal's voluminous work; so much had to be omitted in order to achieve a book of reasonable length!

My first encounter with Cahal's legendary intellectual stature was as a student in the Department of Scholastic Philosophy in Queen's University, Belfast, where he was affectionately known as 'CB'. In whatever capacity he was called to serve God – as scholar, as writer, as theological expert, as moral teacher, as preacher, as Church leader – Cahal was inspired by a profound commitment to serve God selflessly and with complete dedication. One illustration of this selflessness is the fact that, despite having suffered a serious heart attack in February 1982, he accepted 'after days of anxiety and apprehension' the decision of Pope John Paul II that he should become bishop of Down and Connor, remembering the words of St Augustine to the effect that God does not demand the impossible; whatever he commands, he gives the grace to make it possible.

The main text in this book is from the writings and addresses of Cardinal Daly. As much as possible, the stylistic choices of the original texts, such as spelling, capitalisation and punctuation, have been retained. The text in italics is comment by me, which is designed to help the reader by placing the material in context.

I am very grateful to the team in Veritas – Síne Quinn, Maura Hyland, David Macken, Jeannie Swan and Lir Mac Cárthaigh – for their initiation of this project and for their unfailing support throughout its development.

The work could not have been completed without Frances Doran, who had been personal secretary to the then Bishop Daly in Down and Connor from 1982 until 1990 and who remained his friend until his death. I am most grateful to Frances, who responded enthusiastically when asked to type the text – a task she completed with typical efficiency and speed. More importantly, from her deep knowledge of the work of Cahal Daly, she sought to ensure that significant insights were not overlooked.

I am grateful to Archbishop Paul Richard Gallagher, secretary for relations with states and international organisations in the Holy See's Secretariat of State, for permission to publish the address he gave in Belfast to mark what would have been Cahal Daly's one hundredth birthday.

I am also grateful for permission from John Monaghan of Shanway Press who published the address.

I have tried in advance of publication to contact the families of those victims at whose funerals Cahal preached the homilies, which are recorded in chapter 1. I apologise to those for whom I was unable to obtain contact details.

In his book *Steps on my Pilgrim Journey*, published in 1998 by Veritas Publications, Cardinal Daly stated that his last prayer would be the same as St Paul's: 'Life to me is not a thing to waste words on, provided that when I finish my race I have carried out the mission the Lord Jesus gave me – and that was to bear witness to the Good News of God's grace' (Acts 20:24). And he concluded, 'I pray, and I would like my friends to pray, that my life might have been such as not to belie these words.'

I invite all who read this book to join in that prayer for Cardinal Daly and for all Christians.

Gemma Loughran

INTRODUCTION

At a Mass in the Pro-Cathedral in Dublin on 14 October 2001, Cardinal Cahal Daly spoke about the Good Friday Agreement:

> A new vision for Ireland was sketched in the Good Friday Agreement. This was endorsed by the people in a country-wide referendum, in which, for the first time since 1918, the inhabitants of the whole island voted. By a very large majority, people North and South subscribed to a new understanding about what freedom and unity mean in today's Ireland, an understanding which, for the very first time, secured the assent of North and South, nationalist and unionist inhabitants of the island together. The Agreement is not just visionary; it is founded on a penetrating analysis of the realities which constitute Northern Ireland. There is no other basis on which Northern Ireland can enjoy peace, prosperity and normal life.

Let me avail of this opportunity to say that we in Northern Ireland owe a deep debt of gratitude to the successive governments in Dublin and to their officials for their hard and patient work in the protracted negotiations which eventually culminated in the drawing up of the Good Friday Agreement and in its implementation.

Nationalists now no longer see Irish unity as absorption of a unionist minority into a united Ireland by virtue of an all-island nationalist majority. That crude majoritarian concept of democracy has been relegated to the past; it did not work in Northern Ireland; it will not work in reverse in a unified Ireland. Unionists too have rights. Unionists too have legitimacy in this island. Democracy demands that their rights, and their identity be respected. The Irish majority neither wishes to nor could absorb into itself an unreconciled, unwilling and recalcitrant unionist community. No one should wish to see the negative aspects of Northern Ireland's past repeated in an all-Ireland context. As Cardinal Conway memorably asked, at the very beginning of the Northern 'Troubles'; thirty years ago: 'Who in their sober senses would want to bomb a million Protestants into a united Ireland?'

A united Ireland remains a legitimate and a noble ideal. But the people of this island have repudiated physical force or coercion as a means to attain it. It can be attained only by persuasion, not by force; only by consent, not by constraint; only by creating conditions and building relationships which make its attainment no longer repellent for unionists but acceptable and even attractive for them. Reunification

> is now seen as inseparably linked with two balancing concepts, namely, Unionist consent in the future, and a genuinely new Northern Ireland of equality and partnership in the present.
>
> Indeed, the possibilities of an agreed united Ireland in the future are actually being tested now by the willingness of both political communities to create together in equal partnership an agreed Northern Ireland in the present.
>
> Implementing all aspects of the Good Friday Agreement means being prepared to work for a reconciled Northern Ireland of equality between traditions and justice for all; a Northern Ireland freed from the scandal of sectarianism, at peace within its borders but in structured partnership with its neighbours; a Northern Ireland where the allegiance of its unionist inhabitants to their British identity and of its nationalist inhabitants to their Irish identity are freely and fully respected.

Twenty-five years after the signing of the Good Friday Agreement, those words ring out as a challenge to all – politicians, church members, society at large.

The Right Rev. the Lord Robin Eames of Armagh, who, during six years of Cahal's leadership of the Catholic Church, was Church of Ireland archbishop of Armagh and primate of All Ireland described Cahal as 'one of the great influences on the peace process' whom 'history will applaud [for] what he achieved, through great courage and firm attitude, in human rights and justice issues'.

Most Reverend Joseph Duffy, a former bishop of Clogher, described Cahal Daly as 'commanding major influence as a commentator on the political scene' and as having a 'unique talent for the written word which he communicated day in and day out to the mass media as well as directly to his flock'.

The issues on which Cardinal Daly spoke and wrote ranged from the philosophical, to the theological, to the religious, to the political, to the social, to the pastoral, to the liturgical. This book reflects some of his thoughts on some of these issues.

However, he always insisted that in our culture the only statement that cannot be refuted by a contradictory statement is the statement of a person's life. For him, faithful commitment to Christ is what makes Christ real as no words will ever do; it is what demonstrates the truth of Christ's gospel as learned homilies, books and arguments alone will never do.

CHAPTER 1

The Victims of Violence: Speaking About Their Deaths and Visiting Their Homes

During his service as bishop and cardinal, Cahal Daly spoke about many of the violent deaths in Northern Ireland, often preaching at the funerals of those who had been murdered and visiting the homes of those who mourned them. He described such involvement as 'a heart-breaking Via Dolorosa through homes devastated by grief and anguish'.

The following selection of extracts from his homilies and statements reflects the spectrum of victims in Northern Ireland.

Funeral Mass for Judge William Doyle, 18 January 1983

Judge William Doyle was shot dead by the Irish Republican Army (IRA) on 16 January 1983 as he sat in his car after attending Mass in St Brigid's Church, Belfast, about to give a lift home to a family friend.

Words on such a day as this seem so inadequate. They are inadequate first to express our sympathy with the stricken family, with Judge Doyle's widow, Frances, with his daughters Elizabeth and Frances, with his relatives and friends, with his colleagues in the judiciary and the legal profession, with the people of St Brigid's still reeling from the shock of this godless deed. But our sympathy is deep, with a depth beyond words. It is, as the word itself conveys, a suffering with them; for we suffer at what is being done to our society and by members of our own community; for having come from us, they are not of us. By their words of hate and their policies of murder they cut themselves away from the community of love which is the Christian Church.

Atonement

Words are inadequate too to express our abhorrence of this foul deed. It is doubly a blasphemy against God. First of all, it blasphemes Him in its desecration of human life, created in God's image and likeness, created through love and for love. St John, the beloved disciple, wrote:

> Anyone who … hates his brother is still in the dark. But anyone who loves his brother is living in the light … unlike the man who hates his brother and is in the darkness, not knowing where he's going, because it is too dark to see. (1 Jn 2:9-11)

> This is the message as you heard it in the beginning: that we are to love one another; not to be like Cain, who belonged to the Evil One and cut his brother's throat; cut his brother's throat simply for this reason, that his own life was evil and his brother lived a good life. (1 Jn 3:11-12)

This deed is a blasphemy against God with a note of specific horror because it was a desecration of a holy place, a profanation of a holy time. It arouses our detestation as an inhuman act. It should arouse our revulsion even more as a godless act, an act of sacrilege against God's dwelling place which is the Church building, and against God's holy temple which is the body of the Christian; most evidently so when he is coming from the supreme act of Christian faith and worship which is the Eucharist and from the touch of the holy hand of God in Holy Communion. As Christians we experience a sense of fear and trembling at this insult to the awesome majesty of the Most High God. Let us ponder deeply on the specific evil of such a deed of godlessness. Let us fear for what it can do to our Catholic community, to our Christian faith. Let us pray with deep feeling: 'Lord, deliver us from evil.'

When God's people in biblical times were confronted with this kind of blasphemous evil, they were exhorted by the prophets to expiate the evil and to make atonement and reparation for such crimes to the insulted Divine Majesty. They were to do this by prayer, penance and fasting. As God's people today, we must obey this injunction. Consequently, here in St Brigid's Church, on next Friday, day of the supreme sacrilege of all history which was the killing of the Son of God, there shall be some hours set aside for personal and public prayer in expiation of this evil deed. All who can do so are invited to join in this prayer in the divine Eucharistic presence, to express in Christian fashion our abhorrence of this sacrilegious murder. Those who wish to do so may feel moved to deny themselves one meal in sign of fasting on that same day and could make a donation to some charitable organisation, some work of reconciliation, some service to jobless youth.

The All-Merciful God

But no word of anger or bitterness must sully this Eucharist or Friday's prayer. However great the power of evil, it is never beyond the measure of the length and breadth, the height and the depth of God's love and mercy. I pray and I ask you to pray that these killers may be reached by God's voice in their conscience, may hear His call to repentance, may be converted from sinful ways and turn to God and have their sins, their heinous sins, forgiven. Heart-rending though the grief of widow and daughters and friends, it is better to be victim of such a deed than to be its perpetrator. It is a terrible thing to walk away from the light of Christ into the dark and be alone with one's guilt. Let no one be in any doubt: we must choose between light and darkness, the light of love and the darkness of hate. We must choose between Christ and anti-Christian deeds like that of last Sunday. May those who have chosen against Christ return to Him, 'that they may find mercy and find grace in their time of need' (Heb 4:16).

Menace to Catholicism

May no Catholic harbour any illusions about the menace posed to our faith by such movements as those which plan and order and perpetrate deeds like this. Let no lies confuse them. Let no propaganda deceive them. The present and protracted campaign of violence is, I believe, the gravest danger which has been created for Belfast Catholicism for half a century. It is a force for corruption from within, far greater than any external danger. I pray, and I ask you to pray: 'Lord, deliver us from evil. ... Deliver us, Lord, from every evil and grant us peace in our day.'

Work for Peace

In this Eucharist, where we experience how God has loved us and taken our own sins away, and become Himself our peace, we commit ourselves once more to work for peace and reconciliation. Catholics and Protestants together, we commit ourselves to work for justice through peace and for peace through justice. Our belief in peace is unshaken. Our hope for peace is irrepressible. [Philosopher Emmanuel] Mounier defined Christian hope as a blend of pity, patience and stubbornness. With all the stubbornness of the North we, Catholics and Protestants, shall believe in peace, pray for peace, work for peace. And we shall overcome. We shall not 'be overcome by evil, but overcome evil by good'. Let us not forget that the most awful thing that could happen in human history has already happened. It happened on that dark Friday when they crucified the Son of God. But that day is also Good Friday; because in defeat Christ conquered; 'dying He destroyed our death'. He is risen, He is alive, He is with us. He says to us:

> In the world you shall have distress, but have confidence, I have overcome the world. (Jn 16:33)

At his Ascension, as we read in the Acts of the Apostles, the disciples were 'staring into the sky' when the Angels said to them:

> Why are you ... standing here looking into the sky? Jesus ... will come back in the same way as you have seen Him go [into heaven]. (Acts 1:11)

It was as though to say: do not stand around indulging in self-pity; there is work to do for Christ before He comes back.

My dear brothers and sisters in Christ, Catholics and Protestants together, we have work to do for Christ before He comes again: a work of love; a work of peace; a work of healing; a work of justice. Let us set to it. Peace is possible, if we want it, if we pray for it, if we are willing to make sacrifices for it; if we build bridges of understanding; if we erect structures and institutions of justice. 'With God, all things are possible.' So we shall together struggle stubbornly on 'helped by God's power driving us all irresistibly'.

Funeral Mass for Mary Travers, 11 April 1984

Mary Travers, a Catholic teacher aged twenty-two, was shot dead by the IRA on 8 April 1984 outside St Brigid's Church, Belfast, while leaving Mass with her father, Tom, a resident magistrate. At that time, she was the fourth person to have been murdered since the beginning of the Troubles while leaving Mass – two of them victims of loyalists, two of them victims of republicans.

The family at Bethany was one where Jesus was a familiar presence and a dear friend. We are told, 'Jesus loved Martha and her sister [Mary] and Lazarus.' How like the Travers family. Jesus was always a living presence in their home, as real to them as they were to one another, and even more loved. Tom and his wife, Joan, and their children, Tom, Martin, Paul, Hugh, Mary and Ann, were a happy, loving family, united in their love for one another and in their faith and prayer.

The last Gospel that Mary was to hear read in her mortal life – the account of the raising of Lazarus from the dead in the eleventh chapter of St John – was finally not a Gospel of sorrow but of happiness, not a story of death, but of resurrection and glory. Hearing of Lazarus' sickness, Jesus said:

> This sickness will end, not in death, but in God's glory, and through it the Son of God will be glorified.

So has it been in this tragedy and in Mary's death. God's glory has been shown by it. The Son of God has been glorified by it. All who have met the family during these days will know that one has met the living Lord, present in the midst of their grief. The faith of the family and their spirit of loving forgiveness even and especially of those who did this brutal deed, have shown that Jesus Christ indeed lives and is with us to the end of time. Deep though the family's sadness over Mary, they feel a still deeper sadness that any human beings could be capable of doing this awful thing to their child.

Mary had taken up her first teaching post only six months ago in Holy Child Boys' School. She loved those children. She wanted never to teach in any other school. She wished, more than anything else, to bring her love and her care to those little boys of Andersonstown and to their mothers and fathers. Her death is a tragic blow to the people of Andersonstown to whom she wanted to give her young life and her great talents and her warm and loving personality. Colleagues describe her as one who radiated goodness and innocence.

I sympathise with the teachers of Holy Child School and with all the other members of the school services, and with the children and the parents, in their loss of such a friend. I want to sympathise with the teachers of West Belfast and indeed their colleagues everywhere, and to express my admiration of the way they have kept the virus of violence out of school life and have made their schools oases of peace and places of love during the years in which violence raged around them and the love of many had grown cold and some hearts around them had turned to stone.

Mary was preparing to go on Sunday afternoon to St Agnes' church for the first confession of her class. She had prepared the music, practised the hymns and the prayers, and was hurrying to share the joy of her little ones in coming for the first time to the sacrament of God's loving reconciliation of us with Himself and with one another. The simple and innocent prayers of those little ones follow Mary now, as she herself 'follows the Lamb wherever he goes' (Rv 14:4). Our Lord said:

> Let the little children come to me and do not stop them, for it is to such as these that the kingdom of heaven belongs. (Mt 19:14)

In another place, Jesus said:

> Unless you change and become like little children, you will never enter the kingdom of heaven. (Mt 18:3)

Surely it is to such as Mary that the kingdom of heaven belongs.

All the Catholic teachers and school children and many parents of West Belfast will be assisting at special Masses this morning to pray for Mary's soul, for her father's recovery, for the comforting of the shocked family and for peace. I ask all Catholics in the diocese to redouble their prayers in these last days of Lent and through Holy Week for these intentions and for the repentance and forgiveness of Mary's killers, and to offer atonement to Almighty God for all the heinous murders of the past years. The liturgy and adoration of the Blessed Sacrament on Holy Thursday and the liturgy of Good Friday and the beautiful liturgy of the Easter Vigil are especially suitable for this prayer and reparation.

That Your Sins May Be Forgiven

Not a single word of anger or of bitterness or of condemnation has passed the lips of the family of Mary Travers since this terrible happening. Today, no word of anger or denunciation shall pass our lips. We shall only ask the killers, as the sight of the pain-wracked bodies of their victims comes before their eyes, to see there Jesus dying on his Cross, his body twitching with the spasms of his pain. It is he who speaks to them: 'So long as you did this to one of these my little ones, you did it to me.'

How I wish I could speak to those who sent the perpetrators out to kill on that peaceful Sunday morning in spring. How I wish I could speak to those who fired those murderous guns. How I wish that you would listen at least not to me, but to the voice of Christ. There is no need to say that what you have done is most grievously sinful. Please stop trying to deceive yourselves any more with propaganda. When you stand before the God of truth, there will be no place for cant. You will see then for what they really are the lies you have been fed, and the brainwashing which led you to Sunday morning's blood. When you joined this organisation, you never thought that you would end up murdering an innocent girl on her way home from Mass, hurrying to prepare young boys from Andersonstown for their first Confession. You are victims just as much as poor Mary was. You do yourselves far more harm than you did to her.

But you don't need to go on doing it. You don't even need to carry the shame and the guilt of it to your grave. You did this in the Holy Season of Lent, approaching the greatest of Christian feasts, the feast of Easter. Lent is for you too. It is your time, it is your chance, to repent and to be forgiven. Come to your priests. Come to me if you wish. I promise you, you will find only Christ's love and forgiveness and the offer from Christ of a totally new beginning.

Mary taught young children. I want to speak now to the parents of young children. Pray that your children may never be caught up in organisations that plan and do these dreadful things. Never allow the poison of hatred to enter the hearts of your children by any word or attitude of your own. Avoid those who foster hatred in your community: deeds of murder stem from words and feelings of hate.

To young people, I want to say: it is sinful to join organisations which train you and order you to do awful deeds such as those of last Sunday. It is sinful to remain in these organisations. It is sinful to entice others to join them. If you had any illusions left about a 'glorious cause' or a heroic 'armed struggle', you cannot have them any longer. Now is the time to get out. Now is the time to start a new life. Now is the time to begin to work with peaceful passion for real justice and through justice, peace.

Political Organisations Supporting Violence

I should wish to speak directly to the leaders of the political organisation which calls for 'unambiguous support' for the campaign of which last Sunday's slaughter is part. You claim to be concerned about social issues and about justice for your constituents. Mary Travers worked to give a proper start in life and the hope of a better future to the children of Andersonstown, one of the communities that you claim to wish to 'liberate'. Surely you will have the integrity and the honesty, the courage and the compassion now to denounce her murder and repudiate those who did it and disassociate yourselves unambiguously from the organisation which coldly planned this deed and sent out the perpetrators.

I should wish to speak to people who have supported this political organisation in the past. I ask you to reflect now on the true nature of a so-called 'armed struggle', which at point-blank range shoots a young girl, falling back dead into the arms of her mother, and which pours bullets at arm's length into her father, lying in her blood and in his, but thinking and speaking not of himself but of Mary. I ask you to judge this organisation and its leaders and its representatives by what they will say now about Mary Travers' death. I ask you to remember Mary Travers and her love for the children of Andersonstown. Remember her if people who refuse to condemn her murder ask you later to vote for them.

Tom Travers is still critically ill. I wish to express my admiration and the gratitude of all of us to the surgeons and the theatre staffs of Belfast City Hospital, who have worked with such dedication and skill, night and day since Sunday, to save his life. I wish to express the appreciation of all of us to the staff of the City Hospital who, at all levels, have shown such care and concern to all of Tom's family and their friends. We assure Mrs Travers and her family that we pray for his continuing and complete recovery. We have had many messages of prayer from our fellow-Christians of different communions, and we thank them for this expression of Christian brotherhood at this time of common trial.

May this sad event be a turning point for all of us. May it be a call to conversion for every sector of society. May it end at last all ambivalence and equivocation about support for the so-called 'armed struggle'. No cause can ever justify murder.

Those who condone murder by refusing to condemn it lose all right to speak of justice.

May the prayers of Mary, Mother of Jesus, be with you, Mrs Travers, and your husband and your daughter and sons, to support you in this great sorrow. She watched her Son die and received his dead body in her arms from the Cross. But first Jesus had given her to you and to us as our Mother: 'This is your mother,' he said. We pray to her with you and for you:

> Mother of Sorrows, pray for us.
> Consoler of the Afflicted, pray for us.
> Queen of Peace, pray for us.

Funeral Mass for Martin Duffy, 22 July 1986

Martin Duffy, aged twenty-eight, was a married man and the father of three children. He worked as a fireman and part-time taxi-driver. He was shot dead by loyalists on 19 July 1986 on the Antrim Road in Belfast as he responded to what is believed to have been a bogus call to pick up a fare.

No matter how often one kneels by the coffin of a young murdered man, one never becomes inured to the heartbreak of it. In the past years, I have knelt by the coffins of many who died violent deaths – young RUC [Royal Ulster Constabulary] men, young Catholic victims of sectarian hatred, young men killed by IRA or INLA [Irish National Liberation Army] gunmen, a young man killed by an RUC plastic bullet. There is no political colouring on tears, be they Catholic or Protestant. There are no denominational differences to distinguish hearts broken by grief.

Kneeling by the open coffin of Martin Duffy one experiences shock and sorrow and a sense of desolation; one is overcome by a feeling of shame that people can bring themselves to do this evil thing to their fellow-man. One touches with trembling what St Paul calls the 'mystery of iniquity' (2 Th 2:7). The words of the prayer Our Lord taught us come to one's lips: 'Deliver us from evil.'

But one feels touched also by the immense compassion of Christ, who enters into the depths of human sorrow and even takes upon himself the sins of the world, which are the ultimate source of all human sorrow. Out of the depths of our heartbreak, he cries to the Father on our behalf for pity, for forgiveness, for healing. By the coffin of Martin Duffy, we think of Jesus standing by the grave of Lazarus, his friend, and sighing with the grief of the grieving sisters and friends of the deceased. St John tells us that Jesus was 'in great distress' and sighed 'with a sigh that came straight from the heart' (Jn 11:33).

My dear Rosemary, Martin's wife; dear Kevin, Martine and Michael, his children; dear John and Agnes, his father and mother; dear John, Joe, Tommy, Paul and Patrick, his brothers, and all Martin's friends, especially his dear friend Jim, the same Jesus is among you now, sharing your grief, putting his comforting and supporting arms around you, and promising you that he is with you through it all. I offer you my heartfelt sympathy and assure you of my prayers, as do all the people in this church in this time of your deepest sorrow. In the beautiful words of today's liturgy: 'May the faith be your consolation and eternal life your hope.'

Martin was known to his friends and his acquaintances, his neighbours and his colleagues, as a universally popular and obliging and cheerful young man, always ready to do a good turn for anyone who needed help. As a fireman, a member of a distinguished service to which the community owes so much and of which the whole community should be so proud, Martin, in the best tradition of the Service, came to the help of all, regardless of creed or politics, and showed courage way beyond the line of duty in saving lives, without pausing to ask whether they were Protestant or Catholic. He had no political involvements and no sympathy with violence in any form. He lived for his home, his wife and children and family, and for his work. He brought cheerfulness and pleasure to all with whom his work as fireman or as taxi driver for Cedar Taxis brought him in contact. He was a Catholic and this was the only reason why he was killed.

Not 'Protestant Killers'

But let us not call his murderers 'Protestant killers'. The name 'Protestant' is the name of an honourable religious tradition which has enriched history and which stands for all that is best and noblest in the beliefs and values and lives of millions of Christians. The true Protestant tradition abjures hatred and abhors murder. It fears God and honours human life as sacred. It proclaims the Christian Gospel of love and forgiveness, of tolerance and reconciliation. The term 'Protestant killers' is an abuse of the Protestant name and insult to the community of true Protestant Christians. Genuine Protestants deplore and condemn murders like that of Martin Duffy as unreservedly as any Catholic could.

The welcome presence of many Protestants at our funeral liturgy today, whether from the Fire Service or from Martin's taxi firm or from other walks of life, witnesses to that truth. The fact that one of the lessons of our liturgy today was read by a Protestant and that Protestant colleagues from both of

Martin's workplaces are paying their respects to him in the course of our religious service, is itself an indication that bigotry does not have the last word in our community and that evil does not and will not triumph.

Church Leadership

Churchmen must set the example for politicians in the clarity of their proclamation of God's law and in the courage of their stand against violence, particularly violence which is perpetrated in the name of the community of which they have pastoral care. I believe that churchmen must be careful not to speak to or for one political community only, but must endeavour to be aware of the impact which their words will have on the other political community as well. Churchmen must try to speak across the barriers dividing the two communities. No less is demanded of the ministers of reconciliation which Christian pastors are called to be at all times, and particularly at this point in our history.

We churchmen must make ourselves informed about the fears and feelings and perceptions of religious communities other than our own. We must recognise, and help our people to recognise, the rights and the grievances, the aspirations and the sensitivities and the hurt memories of other religious communities. In this way we can set a headline for politicians, and this is both our Christian duty and our country's need: for it is clear that only our Christian faith can lighten a way through our present darkness to a future where political murder and sectarian murder alike shall be banished from our land, and there will no more mourning and sadness like that of the stricken Duffy family today.

False Defenders

But both communities must be alert to the fact that there are in their midst people who have a political interest in perpetuating violence. There are people, both loyalist and republican, whose strategy dictates that it is only through the sufferings of communities that political ends can be achieved. There are ideologies which require, as a matter of revolutionary principle, that situations must be deliberately made worse and worse in the present, in order that some alleged 'golden dawn' may break through in some mythical future.

I appeal to Catholics not to listen to paramilitary sympathisers who would pretend to be their defenders, but who in reality would only bring endless further torment upon communities which have endured too long sorrow.

I ask all to pray fervently and to pray unwaveringly for the peace which God alone can grant to us. I am edified by the religious fervour evident among the congregation gathered here and among the people of this parish. I am inspired by the knowledge that so many came to receive the sacrament of reconciliation during these days of grief. The first condition of being reconciled with one another is that we be reconciled with God. I can have no message for you at this time other than the message of St Paul: 'We are ambassadors for Christ. It is as though God were appealing through us, and the appeal we make in Christ's name is: Be reconciled to God' (2 Cor 5:20).

A Week of Murders in June 1987

Bishop Daly released the following statement in response to a series of killings which took place between 23 and 26 June 1987. The

Darkley and Whitecross incidents referred to are the killing of three and wounding of seven worshippers at Mountain Lodge Pentecostal Church at Darkley in Co. Armagh on 20 November 1983, for which the INLA claimed responsibility, and the shooting of three members of the Reavey family by members of the Ulster Volunteer Force (UVF) at their home in Whitecross on 4 January 1976, killing two brothers, John and Brian, and fatally injuring a third, Anthony, aged seventeen.

Northern Ireland has witnessed a cruel history of sectarian murders – the awful multiple killings, for example, at Darkley and Whitecoss, of Protestants killed merely because they were Protestants and the wicked destruction of the lives of Catholics slain simply because they were Catholics.

This week stands out even in our grim times as a week of evil and shame. We had the murder on Tuesday last, 23 June, of RUC Sergeant Robert Guthrie, killed by a gun fired from a children's playground on the Cavehill Road, Belfast, as he arrived for work at Antrim Road police station in his own car. He was a forty-one-year-old Protestant who leaves a widow and two teenage children. We had the murder in Surrey Street, Belfast, on Friday, 26 June, of UDR [Ulster Defence Regiment] Private John Tracey who worked as an electrician. He leaves a widow and six children.

Emmanuel Wilson was shot dead on 24 June in circumstances and in manner most foul by killers who were most probably members of our own community in West Belfast. He leaves a grieving widow, Carol, and four children to whom I offer my deep and prayerful sympathy.

Danny O'Connor, a thirty-year-old who worked as a cook in the Mater Hospital, Belfast, was shot dead on 25 June on the Springfield Road, Belfast, as he unloaded last-minute holiday shopping from his car. He is undoubtedly the innocent victim of sectarian killers, striking fanatically but purposefully at any Catholic whom their gun gang could identify and reach. To his stricken widow, Patricia, and the heartbroken children, I offer my deepest sympathy and prayers.

In this one week alone we have had four women left widowed and sixteen children left orphans.

No Ambivalence About Murder

Let us as Christians examine ourselves on our reaction to these murders. Did we feel differently about them according to whether the victims were Catholic or Protestant? Did we think that some of these murders were wicked, but others were 'justified', or at least 'understandable'? Do we distinguish killings according to political labels, reserving the term 'murder' for killings perpetrated by people of whom we politically disapprove? Do we judge killings by Christ's standards, or do we judge them by the standards of some political cause or movement?

Honesty obliges us to ask how it could ever have come about that people who presumably came from Catholic families and passed through Catholic schools could have so rejected the Christian values in which they were reared as to become capable of doing such a deed as the killing of Emmanuel Wilson.

These questions are crucial ones; they ask whether Christ is really our Lord, or whether his place as Lord of our consciences has been taken over by politics. Are we letting God be our God, or is some political cause taking the place of God in our lives? The first of the Ten Commandments is the one which says:

> I am the Lord your God: you shall not have strange gods before me. (Ex 20:2-3)

The term 'strange gods' does not refer only to the idols of pagan cults. Politics too can become idolatry, the worship of false gods, when it claims to set aside the teaching of Christ and his Church, and make 'the Cause' or 'the Movement', rather than God's commandments, the determinant of our decisions and our moral judgements.

It is with a full sense of my responsibilities as one who has been appointed by the Holy Spirit as bishop in the Church of God in Down and Connor and among the successors of the Twelve Apostles, that I say, not in my own name, but in the name of God and of His Christ: All these killings are mortal sins of murder. The mortal sin of murder is incurred, not only by those who pull the trigger, but by those who order or authorise and those who plan the killing, those who hide the guns, those who freely and knowingly provide the 'safe houses', those who provide information about the victim's address and movements, those who are deliberate accomplices in the crime.

For every person who murders, there are many others in the community who share in the guilt of murder. I pray, and I ask you to pray, that God may touch their hearts and open their eyes to the mortal peril of their immortal souls in which they are living, unless they repent and seek God's forgiveness.

Not Politics but Christ's Teaching

What I am saying has nothing to do with politics. It has to do only with God's law and with the salvation of souls. When I, after whatever short years are now left to me, come before God to give an account to Him of my episcopal ministry, I shall be asked by my eternal Judge whether I faithfully and fearlessly proclaimed His law and whether I put before God's people the whole of His truth, by which alone they can be saved. As the years pass, my concern grows as to how I personally stand as bishop before St Paul's words to the bishops of the Church whom he addressed at Ephesus:

> Be on your guard for you yourselves and for all the flock, of which the Holy Spirit has made you the bishops to feed the Church of God which he bought with his own blood. (Acts 20:28)

Can I hope, at the end of my life, to say what St Paul said:

> Here and now I swear that my conscience is clear as far as all of you are concerned, for I have without faltering put before you the whole of God's purpose. (Acts 20:26-7)

I am not personally responsible for what individual Catholics in my diocese do: that is their decision and their responsibility. But I am personally responsible as bishop for telling them clearly what is God's revealed judgement on what they do; and if I were to leave them in ignorance or confusion or doubt about God's teaching on their conduct, then I should be held responsible by God for my neglect. God said long ago to the prophet Ezekiel:

> Son of man, I have appointed you as watchman to the house of Israel. Whenever you hear a word from me, warn them in my Name ... If you do not speak and warn [the sinner] to renounce his evil ways and so

> live, then he shall die for his sin, but I will hold you responsible for his death. . . . If, however, you warn the upright man not to sin and he abstains from sinning, he shall live, thanks to your warning, and you too will have saved your life. (Ez 3:16-21)

These words stand as a solemn warning to anyone who has teaching responsibility in Christ's Church. Any cleric who, by word or deed, might cause people to have a false or confused conscience about the sinfulness of the so-called 'armed struggle', would be giving grave scandal to Christ's flock and would be taking upon his own soul a truly terrifying responsibility before God.

The Evil of Sectarianism

So far as sectarian murderers are concerned, our society must face up to the fact that sectarian bigotry has been a curse on our society for the past century or more, and continues in some circles to be as virulent as ever. West Belfast has been scourged by sectarianism in generation after generation. It is estimated that the pogroms of the 1920s saw some 30,000 Catholics driven from their homes and places of work and become refugees, many of them crowding into West Belfast. In the 1970s, the most recent great outbreak of this plague of pogroms, it is calculated that as many as 40,000 people, the vast majority of them Catholics, were similarly driven from their homes. Again, many of them found refuge in West Belfast.

A high proportion of the Catholic population of greater West Belfast would have personal experience of attacks by loyalist mobs upon their streets or homes, their own or those of their parents or grandparents, here or in other parts of the city, some of them several times in the memory of one family. There are few phenomena more scandalous for Christians than that of sectarian hatred. It challenges all the Churches and their leaders to speak fearlessly and tirelessly that word of truth which sets us free from false judgement of other faiths, that word of love which sets us free from fear.

It is deeply disturbing that some loyalist spokesmen continue to impute to the whole Catholic community responsibility and guilt for the sins of a very few. Some of them even make a rhetorical equation between Catholic, 'republican' and gunman. I appeal to these spokesmen to reflect on the possible consequences of this deplorable misuse of language. The killers of Danny O'Connor presumably made just that kind of equation. It is essential that leaders of the loyalist community take great care that nothing they say could in any way encourage that sort of attitude.

It is still more reprehensible that, in a small number of Protestant churches, there is poured out from the pulpit, Sunday after Sunday, a stream of vile anti-Roman Catholic abuse and invective. This is totally untypical of the mainstream Protestant Churches. It is an insult to the true Protestant faith. Yet it is a fact of life in some circles in Northern Ireland, to which we must not blind our eyes. Sustained work towards its elimination must be part of the continuing programme of preaching, religious education and pastoral activity of all the Churches.

As for politicians in both communities, it is surely clear that the dangerous situation we are facing, as well as the voices of large numbers of people in both communities, are calling out to them to begin urgently to engage in talks with a view to finding a political way forward. The talks must aim at finding ways whereby unionists can come to understand, respect and accommodate nationalists' rights and aspirations, without betraying their own; and whereby nationalists can come to understand, respect and accommodate unionists' rights and aspirations, without betraying their own. Some say this is impossible. I say it is necessary, if there is ever to be peace between Irishmen; and there must be peace. When the 'impossible' is necessary it becomes a moral duty. And Christians must remember that nothing is impossible for God.

Ulterior Motives for Killings?

In addition to the four successive murders in four days of last week, we also had the attempted murder of a UDR member and the wounding of his mother, impiously shot at from near the Catholic Church grounds at Ligoniel. This is particularly deplorable, in an area where good community relations had been carefully built up over the past and had survived even the troubles of recent years, but are now obviously put under great strain by such barbarous events.

Indeed, this incident at Ligoniel puts the whole Catholic community there at risk. The same could be said about the murder of Sergeant Guthrie at the bottom of the Cavehill Road and the murder of Private Tracey in the Lisburn Road area. The IRA know what are the likely consequences of such deeds for the Catholic communities in this sort of area. Is it their deliberate intention to provoke sectarian strife?

Looking at the pattern of recent IRA activities, and considering their timing, on the eve of the loyalist marching season, and their location, at exposed community interfaces, one has to ask whether this is indeed the ulterior motive. It has been proven by experience that the IRA do not carry out their operations arbitrarily. There is a steel-cold purpose and a calculated political point in every operation. I want publicly today to ask those responsible for the political and the paramilitary leadership of the IRA whether the provocation of sectarian strife is now part of their strategy, and whether exposing Catholic communities to attack is part of their tactic.

Christian Hope

In spite of all that might make for depression and discouragement, we Christians remain men and women of undefeatable hope. We are the people who, as St John puts it, have put our faith in love:

> We ourselves have known and put our faith in God's love towards ourselves. God is love and anyone who lives in love lives in God, and God lives in him. (1 Jn 4:16)

God has shown His love for us supremely through the death of His Son for us on the Cross. Christ died to bring us the only true freedom, which is liberation from the enslaving grip of sin and hatred and the spirit of revenge. Through the death of Christ on Calvary, these evil things have already been defeated, and nothing can defeat our hope that through Christ's Passion and his Cross, we shall experience the glory of his resurrection and our land shall enjoy his peace.

A striking story is told from the days of the 1941 air raids over Belfast. It concerns a German Luftwaffe pilot who took part in the bombing raid on the night of 15 April 1941, and who was later captured by the Allied Forces. He subsequently described the unforgettable impression made upon him as he saw from his bomber plane cockpit the Calvary at

Beechmount, brightly illuminated and dominating the whole Falls Road in the light of the flares dropped from the German aircraft.

Here in the Calvary which stands at the eastern end of St Paul's church, Christ stretches out his arms on the cross-beam of the Cross to embrace in his universal love the Shankill as well as the Falls, while the upright beam of the Cross points to the Universal Father, to whom the dying Christ prays from the Cross: 'Father, forgive them, for they do not know what they are doing.' He died that we might all have peace in him, peace with God through his forgiveness of our sins, peace with our former enemies through our forgiving them and seeking their forgiveness of us.

In this Marian Year, we pray that Mary, who stood by her Son on Calvary, may obtain for us the grace to continue to stand faithfully by her Son and stand bravely against violence and hate, and stand to work steadily for peace. We pray through her:

> Mary, Queen of Peace, obtain for us from your Son his gift of peace.

Funeral Mass for William (Billy) Kane, 18 January 1988

Billy Kane, aged nineteen, was shot dead by loyalists at his home in the New Lodge area of North Belfast on 15 January 1988. His father, Edward Kane, had been killed in an attack on McGurk's Bar in North Belfast on 4 December 1971.

Billy Kane is a Catholic killed merely for being a Catholic – another North Belfast victim of a loyalist attack.

This is in fact the second time that loyalist sectarian hatred has struck the Kane family. Billy's father, Edward, was killed in the bombing of McGurk's Bar in North Queen Street by loyalists in 1971. I offer my heartfelt sympathy to Billy's mother, Bridget, to her husband, David Moss, to Billy's brother, Eddie; to his sisters, Carol and Nicola, who watched in horror along with their mother and two little grandchildren as the murderers did their infamous deed. I offer deep sympathy also to Billy's girlfriend, Roisin McAree. I offer sincere sympathy also to the neighbours of Upper Meadow Street and the whole New Lodge neighbourhood, who have shared in the shock and grief of the Kane and Moss home, and who have been so supportive of the family in their tragic loss. I offer sympathy in particular to the young men friends of Billy, who feel in a specially poignant way the death of a cheerful and popular companion.

Sectarian History

Sectarian inter-community feuding has been a plague afflicting urban society in Belfast for most of the city's history. Reading Dr Ambrose Macaulay's masterly book on *Patrick Dorrian, Bishop of Down and Connor from 1865 to 1885* [Irish Academic Press, 1987], one is struck by the melancholy thought of how little has changed in terms of inter-community relationships in what are technically called 'working class' areas in Belfast. Already Andrew Boyd, in his book *Holy War in Belfast* [Pretani Press, 1987], had authoritatively detailed the sad chronicle of sectarian conflicts over nearly a century and a half. The dark list of riots, pogroms and bigoted sermons and speeches stretches from 1857 through 1864, 1872, 1886, 1893, 1912, 1920 to 1922, 1935, right up to our own time.

This history is both a rebuke and a challenge to all the Christian Churches in our land. This scandal of sectarianism must be faced resolutely and combated vigorously by the clergy of all denominations. The deformations of religion, the inherited prejudices and misconceptions and even superstitions about one another's beliefs, the sheer religious ignorance and the persistence of plain religious bigotry which lie behind this deplorable history must be courageously identified and perseveringly corrected.

The Week of Prayer for Christian Unity, which began yesterday, 17 January, and continues until next Sunday, 24 January, must not be just a polite annual display of conventional courtesy. It must be for all committed Christians a time of fervent prayer together for mutual understanding and Christian love, a time of examination of conscience, of repentance and conversion, as we seek to bring before God and before one another for forgiveness the sins against Christian love which lurk in our own personal and community attitudes. I ask Catholics to attend in particularly large numbers this year at the ecumenical services arranged for the week, and thus to demonstrate the commitment of the Catholic community to seek dialogue, friendship and reconciliation with their Protestant brother and sister Christians, with whom they wish to share this land in peace and partnership.

Religious Discrimination

Responsibility for eliminating inter-community hostility and strife does not, however, rest solely with the Churches. All interests in our society, government, local councils, political parties, professional associations, employers' organisations and trade unions, all have a responsibility to combat sectarianism and religious discrimination. One of the major tasks of government must be to place beyond all doubt or suspicion their commitment to fair employment. There must be credible and effective structures and efficacious legislation, backed by appropriate sanctions, to ensure the elimination, within a reasonable timescale, of all religiously discriminatory practices from employment and from the workplace.

Sensitivity by Security Forces

The deployment and demeanour of the security forces must be kept under rigorous review. There have been allegations, which carry the ring of credibility, about insensitive behaviour by security forces in the New Lodge area in the immediate aftermath of the Billy Kane murder. Indeed, there is widespread perception in areas like New Lodge of a propensity on the part of security forces to single out young men for constant interception, interrogation and rough treatment.

Any fair-minded person must admit that policing in certain areas is rendered inordinately difficult by the ever-present danger to life and limb from IRA attack to which the security forces are exposed, and from the regular provocation of security forces personnel which is part of IRA policy. Nevertheless, it is high time that police and army planners should have devised methods of selecting and training specialised personnel, endowed with the sensitivity, the understanding of local community feelings and attitudes, and the particular skills which are required for effective and sensitive professional policing in flashpoint areas. In such areas, very much more is required than ordinary police training and techniques. Unless there is sensitive and sympathetic awareness of local community traditions and feelings and mentalities, police tactics can defeat the very purpose for which they are intended and can become a factor positively helping the subversive strategy and propaganda of paramilitary organisations. There has been significant and highly praiseworthy progress in the area of impartial and professional policing over recent years. In middle class areas, on the whole, policing is now accepted as an impartial, courteous, efficient and helpful service to the public. There is a great task still to be accomplished before the same perception is achieved in 'working class' nationalist areas.

Let us not forget today, however, that two other families have been bereaved this weekend. Off-duty UDR soldiers Timothy David Armstrong and William John Stewart were also callously murdered. Another mother and father are in mourning, another girlfriend is plunged into shock and grief, just like Roisin. Another Catholic man is very seriously ill in Downpatrick, after an attempted assassination. Murders are no less detestable and despicable, no matter what the religion or affiliation of the victim. There are no 'legitimate targets' in our society. Murders of UDR men or RUC men are directly responsible for provoking loyalist backlash against innocent Catholics.

Let there be no illusions. The paramilitaries who pose as defenders of Catholic enclaves are instead a major cause of the sufferings of Catholic communities. If they were to cease their activity, the heavy security presence and heavy-handed security activity would cease and loyalist paramilitary murders would rapidly be brought to an end. My dear people, peace is the only way to true protection and steady progress towards justice for Catholic communities. Peace is the Christian way, peace is Christ's way to justice. Peace is what Christ offers us in this Eucharist. Peace is the mark of a Eucharistic community.

> Always be wanting peace with all people, and the holiness without which no one can ever see the Lord. Be careful that no one is deprived of the grace of God and that no root of bitterness should begin to grow and make trouble; this can poison a whole community. And be careful … that any of you does not degrade religion. (Heb 12:14-16)

'Root of bitterness' is a very striking phrase. St James says that it is from 'the passions fighting inside our own selves' that all wars and battles first start (cf. Jas 4:11). Until we try to take bitterness and anger out by the root from our own hearts and our own lives, we shall be, even though we may not wish to be, contributing to violence in society and violence between communities. This is a difficult and painful process. In moments of great hurt and in presence of grave wrong it can seem impossible. But if we open our hearts to let Christ into them then he will remove the 'root of bitterness' in us and make us instead 'rooted and founded in love' (cf. Eph 3:17). Remember always the words of Christ which are the central words of our Eucharist: 'This is my body given up for you. This is my blood … [which] will be shed for you and for all so that sins may be forgiven'. The sins for which Christ offered his life in atonement included particularly the sins of those who crucified him. St Paul pleads with us: 'Forgive one another as God has forgiven you in Christ' (Eph 4:32). Before receiving Our Lord in holy communion, we pray together the Our Father, and ask God to 'forgive us our trespasses as we forgive those who trespass against us'. We are thereby making our own forgiveness of those who do us wrong a condition for our receiving forgiveness ourselves from God. That is a very heavy and solemn responsibility which we take upon ourselves, we who ourselves have so much need of forgiveness from God.

Hope of Eternal Life

At this funeral Mass, we come before God chiefly to declare our faith in life everlasting and to renew our hope of being with Christ forever. Billy, aged only twenty years, hoping for marriage and with the promise of a long life stretching out before him, was shot dead as he slept. It was a moment of appalling shock for his loved ones who looked on helplessly at the awful deed. For Billy too it was a moment of shock; but it was a different kind of shock, a delighted shock, the shock of seeing the blessed vision of God in glory. I think of the words of Psalm 16:

> As for me, ... I shall see your face and be filled, when I awake, with the sight of your glory. (Ps 16:15)

Death is in fact not the closing of one's eyes, but the opening of those eyes forever to the reality of the God whom we have known, to whom we have prayed, whom we have tried to love, and to the truth of the Eucharist, to which we have tried to be faithful. Already, before the full revelation and pledge of everlasting life given us by Christ, Job expressed this hope:

> I know that my Redeemer lives and that he will raise us up last, on the dust of the earth. After my awakening, he will set me close to him, and from my flesh I shall look on God. He whom I shall see will take my part: my eyes will be gazing on no stranger. (Job 19:25-7)

In times of darkness like the present, let us think of Mary, standing near the Cross of her Son as darkness covered the earth on Good Friday. She knew what it was to receive the blood-stained body of her young Son into her arms, just as Bridget and Carol and Nicola did on Friday evening. She knows what they are feeling. She knows all the pain and anguish and desolation of the violent death of a loved one. At moments like this, St Bernard told us, we must 'look at the Star, call upon Mary'. In the words of St Bernard's prayer, the *Salve Regina*, we pray now to Mary for comfort and protection, we implore her intercession for peace:

> After this our exile, show unto us the blessed fruit of thy womb, Jesus.

Funeral Mass for John Devine, 26 July 1989

John Devine, a thirty-seven-year-old married father of three children, was a Catholic. He was shot dead by loyalists in his own home on Fallswater Street, West Belfast. The gunmen forced their way into the house and murdered Mr Devine in the presence of his thirteen-year-old son.

Since I came to Down and Connor as bishop there have been, in this diocese alone, many sectarian murders of innocent Catholics by loyalist killers and I have personally officiated at many of their funerals and have, regrettably, unavoidably missed other funerals.

John Devine had no involvement with any political or paramilitary organisation. He was devoted to his own family and his large and close-knit extended family, his work and his workmates, his darts and his dart-playing friends. His family are devoutly religious and are deriving great strength and comfort from their faith and from daily Mass and Holy Communion and their prayers during these days of tragedy and heartbreak.

This latest murder is a particularly gruesome one. It is frightening that loyalist gunmen can drive right into the heart of a Catholic street off the Falls Road for their evil purpose and drive out again. Why was poor John selected as their victim? It would seem as though any Catholic in that street would have been seen by them as a target for murder and that John's was the first house to which they came with its front door open.

The horror was increased by the fact that John was ruthlessly and repeatedly shot in head and chest, sitting on his favourite armchair in the corner of his living room, before the eyes of his thirteen-year-old son, Sean, while his wife, Marian, and the two other children, Ursula (aged ten) and Aidan (aged two), were away on a day trip to the Glens of Antrim.

My dear Marian, our hearts go out in sympathy and in prayer to you and to Sean, Ursula and little Aidan. For me it was touching to the point of tears on Monday and again on Tuesday to see your son Sean standing by your side to support and comfort you, a young boy exposed to murderous hate so early in his life and yet a brave little man, so adult, so mature, so protective of you in this tragedy which has struck your home. It was as though, with his arm around your shoulder, he was saying: 'I'll look after you, mother, I'll be by your side; together we'll come through.' May your son Sean be a comfort to you, Marian, and to Ursula and Aidan too; may you all be kept safe by God's blessing and the blessed Virgin Mary's intercession and by your dear husband's and father's prayers.

Absence of Bitterness

What was so inspiring amid the grief in your home was the complete absence of bitterness or hatred. John was cruelly shot dead as he was reading his newspaper in his armchair, sitting underneath a religious plaque, showing the face of Our Lord and around it the words of a prayer and a blessing:

> May peace be in this house and in the hearts of all who live here.

That peace was in the hearts and the prayers and the longings of the Devine family and their neighbours. It was not in the lives of the murderers. May God touch their hearts too, so that they may repent of their awful deeds and turn their minds to thoughts of peace.

Visit of Bishop Samuel Poyntz

It is unfortunate that the murderers of John Devine and the murderers of other innocent Catholics are called 'Protestant terrorists'. They are not typical of the Protestant community as a whole; they are condemned and repudiated by the immense majority of Protestants; what they do is a contradiction of the Protestant faith and an insult to the Protestant name.

One light which shone out in the darkness of these recent days was the visit paid to the Devine home in Fallswater Street yesterday by Bishop Samuel Poyntz, of the Church of Ireland Diocese of Connor, to comfort the bereaved family and to pray with me and with them in that house of mourning. He expressed to them in the name of the Church of Ireland community, of which he is Bishop, his horror at this crime and the sympathy of himself and his community.

His visit and the warmth and friendliness with which he was received are a beacon of hope in these sombre times.

In turn, I express to him and to other Protestant church leaders and clergy and people my sympathy and the sympathy of the Catholic community with all those in the Protestant community who have been visited by desolation and death inflicted by republican paramilitaries, falsely claiming to act in the name of the nationalist, or even in the name of the Catholic community. The scene in John Devine's home was exactly the same as that witnessed in many a Protestant home, whether of security forces personnel or of civilians, including the most recent victim, Alexander Bell, the RUC Reserve Constable from Ahoghill who died yesterday, following injuries sustained in a vicious car bomb exploded by the IRA near Cushendall two weeks ago. In all such homes and at all such funerals, Protestant or Catholic, the tears are no different, the grief is the same, the same scars and pain continue in the lonely hearts of the widowed mothers and the orphaned children.

Hope

The whole Bible abounds in descriptions of the tribulations and sufferings of God's people throughout history. But it always accompanies them by the repetition of God's guarantee of the final coming of peace. The tears of the Devine family today, the tears of the wake-houses and the gravesides of these past years, recall for us the tears of the people of Israel, described by the prophet Jeremiah, in words which are applied by Matthew's Gospel to the murder of the Holy Innocents:

> A voice is heard in Ramah,
> sadly and loudly lamenting.
> It was Rachel weeping for her children,
> refusing to be consoled
> because they were no more. (Jer 31:15; cf. Mt 2:18)

But this passage is immediately followed in Jeremiah by the words of the Lord:

> Stop your weeping,
> dry your eyes,
> your hardship will be redeemed ...
> There is hope for your descendants. ...
> I must still remember [my people],
> still be deeply moved [for them],
> and let my tenderness yearn over [them]. (Jer 31:16-20)

In the same chapter of Jeremiah the Lord says:

> I have loved you with an everlasting love.
> I am constant in my affection for you. (Jer 31:3)
>
> They left in tears,
> I will comfort them as I lead them back ...
> For I am Father to Israel,
> And Ephraim is my first-born son. ...
> I will turn their mourning into gladness,
> I will comfort them, give them joy after all their
> affliction. (Jer 31:9-13)

This Mass is the fulfilment of these promises, the guarantee of God's tender and constant love for us. This Mass is the sacrifice of the 'new and everlasting covenant' of love which God has made with us. This Mass is God saying to Marian and to Sean and Ursula and Aidan and to all John's family and friends and to all of us gathered here:

> I have loved you with an everlasting love.
> I am constant in my affection for you.

Let us believe in His love. Let us accept His peace and share it and spread it everywhere.

Funeral Mass for Gabriel Mullaly, 1 March 1989

Gabriel Mullaly, who was aged fifty-four, was a Catholic who had been a police officer before his retirement in 1987. His wife, with whom he had six children, died in 1979. He was killed by the IRA on 27 February 1989 when a booby trap bomb attached to his car exploded while he was travelling along North Road in East Belfast.

I offer my heartfelt sympathy to Mr Mullaly's orphaned children. Dear Maria and Paula, Gabriel and Mark, Claire and Gareth, what words could one find that would even in some little way lessen your sorrow and comfort you in your loss and loneliness? Already ten years ago you lost a loving mother. Now, in tragic and cruel circumstances, you are robbed of your dear father too. What words could heal the ache in your hearts? What words could help the whole family circle and Mr Mullaly's many friends and the many people who will miss his kindness and friendship? No words of mine can bring comfort. Only the words of God can bring healing and consolation. St Paul speaks about grieving for the dead. He says:

Ve wish you to be quite certain, brothers and sisters, ıbout those who have died, to make sure you do not grieve about them like the other people who have no hope. We believe that Jesus died and rose again and that it will be the same for those who have died in Jesus. God will bring them with him. … So we shall stay with the Lord forever. (1 Th 4:13-17)

He ends by saying:

Comfort one another with these words. (1 Th 4:18)

Catholic Victims of IRA

I have officiated and preached at the funerals of many Catholics murdered by loyalist paramilitaries. But never forget the scores of Catholics killed by the IRA in these past years.

In the RUC, Mr Mullaly strove impartially to serve both communities and to respect both traditions. He saw in policing an honourable form of service to the community and a way of helping people. He set himself the highest standards of policing as public service. No society can survive without a police service, and attacks upon the police are fundamentally attacks upon society itself. My visit to the orphaned Mullaly family brought to my mind so many RUC widows and orphans whom I have visited over the years of violence, and whose heartbreak I have shared and whose forgiveness I have admired. These are only a few of the hundreds of mourning RUC families of these sad years.

Had Mr Mullaly been murdered when he was still a serving officer of the RUC, he would have been just as innocent a victim as he was on Monday afternoon, two years after he retired.

Sometimes we speak of innocent victims of paramilitary violence, as if there were another category of victims who are not innocent. The killers themselves speak of 'legitimate targets', as distinct from 'civilian casualties'. We must totally reject that use of language. There are no legitimate targets. Loyalists have neither the right nor the justification to kill anyone. The IRA have neither the right nor the authority nor the legitimacy nor the mandate to kill anybody. All their victims are innocent.

In today's funeral liturgy we pray:

> Lord, welcome our brother to paradise
> and help us to comfort one another
> with the assurance of our faith
> until we all meet in Christ
> to be with you and with our brother forever.

But 'the assurance of our faith' does not come easy. The words of Christian comfort can sometimes come too glibly to the lips. We can sometimes speak the words of faith in a way which makes them sound too pat, too facile, too cheap. But faith can be a hard struggle against everything in us and around us which rebels against God's will. St John called faith 'the victory which overcomes the world'. The world is all that rejects God and resists God and says No to God; and that world is all around us, it is also within us. It takes a long, hard and constant slog and struggle to overcome that world and say Yes to God. Faith can be a battlefield; but it is a battle for God and God has guaranteed the victory.

Let us not be too upset when we find it hard to believe and hard to pray and hard to accept God's will. Faith which does not ask to see in the darkness, but which in spite of all darkness believes, can be the most genuine form of faith. Prayer which is a struggle through a desert of dryness can be the prayer most pleasing to God. We may even feel angry with God. We can feel that God has forgotten us, deserted us. Jesus himself cried out on the Cross:

> My God, my God, why have you forsaken me?

Dear sons and daughters of Mr Mullaly, Jesus knows how you are feeling at this moment. He feels the pain in each of your aching hearts. Try to tell him everything you feel, for he understands, he feels it all with you, he shares it with you. Try to 'cast all your troubles on to him, for he has care of you'.

Your grief has been increased by the falsehoods spoken by the IRA about your father. You know that your father was innocent, upright, kind and good; and lies will never take away that knowledge. Your father is one more innocent victim of pitiless violence.

> May God give Gabriel a merciful judgement and
> forgive all his sins.
> May Christ, the Good Shepherd, lead him safely
> home to be at peace with God our Father.
> And may he be happy for ever with all the saints in
> the presence of the eternal king.

CHAPTER 2

The Imperative of Peace, Whatever the Challenges

Part 1: *Praying for Peace, Working for Peace*

On 8 December 1967 Pope Paul VI issued to all people of goodwill an invitation to open 1968 and every succeeding new year with a concentrated effort of prayer for peace. Throughout his years as bishop and cardinal, Cahal Daly delivered an annual address for peace on 1 January, the only exception being in 1973 when illness prevented him from doing so.

His first addresses in 1968 and in 1969 preceded the outbreak of violence in Northern Ireland in August 1969 and that is why one of them – that preached in St Mel's Cathedral, Longford, on 1 January 1969 – is included here. It reflects an abiding theme of Cahal Daly's – the urgency of the call to Christians to seek through prayer and action to create peace with God and reconciliation within the human community at local, national and international levels. Bishop Daly chose Edith Stein as an example of the cruel murder of an innocent person chosen, like untold millions, to die because of her identity as a member of the Jewish community. She offered her life 'as a sacrificial expiation for the sake of true peace', the achievement of which is an intimidating task calling for faith put energetically and heroically at work through love.

Bishop Daly was convinced from the beginning of the Troubles in Northern Ireland that the credibility and relevance of the Church would be judged by many on the basis of its response to those Troubles and their underlying causes.

In addressing the challenge of peace in Northern Ireland, he focused on two main themes: 'the malignant pathology of, on the one hand, revolutionary and paramilitary violence and, on the other hand, militaristic repression' and the need to develop political structures in Northern Ireland that recognised and accommodated as equally valid and equally legitimate both the Irish and the British dimensions. The British dimension is that of 'roughly one million people who have been in this island for more than three hundred years and who form a rightful and permanent part of Irish reality but who owe allegiance to Britain, who profess a British identity [and] claim British citizenship'. The Irish dimension is embodied in the hearts and minds of those who live in Northern Ireland, who also form a rightful part of Irish reality, who see their identity as Irish and who aspire to the eventual reunification of the country.

Those themes are reflected, together with other important themes, in the following addresses.

World Day of Peace Day Address, 1 January 1969, St Mel's Cathedral, Longford

As indicated above, this is the second of the annual addresses by Bishop Daly to mark the World Day of Peace. It predates the outbreak of violence in Northern Ireland in August 1969.

Prayer for peace is a fervent and repeated and persevering appeal to God, the Lord of history, to move people's minds to will and work and plan for the peace God wills for the world. It is prayer based on faith in God's almighty power and infinite wisdom and unlimited love. It is prayer addressed to Him through Jesus Christ, the Son of His love, in whom He is well pleased, whose mediation He cannot refuse.

I wonder whether in some instances nowadays there is a danger that prayer might be made an instrument of social agitation, of political protest, rather than an uplifting of the soul to God in faith and hope. Some acts and some texts of prayer of which one reads might seem to be addressed to the public and the media rather than to God. There is need for us to renew our attitude to prayer by deepening our faith in God and by renewing our practice of prayer.

The efficacy of prayer for peace and reconciliation has for Christians no need of demonstration. But, nevertheless, recent examples of it are inspiring. One of the most noble among the countless nameless victims of the Nazi gas chambers at Auschwitz was Edith Stein. A Jewish woman, Edith Stein was one of the most able as well as one of the favourite disciples of the German philosopher Husserl, who died in the full spate of Nazi persecution, and died himself very near to Christ and the Church. Edith Stein became a Catholic and then became a Carmelite nun, with the name Sister Teresa Benedicta.

It was on 1 January 1939 that her Superiors transferred her to Holland, where it was thought she might be safe from the Nazis. But, of course, the Nazi occupation of Holland followed and in 1942 the Dutch Bishops issued a pastoral letter protesting against Nazi brutalities, especially against the Jews. In hysterical fury the Nazis ordered a further ruthless rounding up of Jews for the gas chamber. Sister Benedicta was among them. She spent a few weeks in Auschwitz, the infamous extermination camp in Poland. On a day in August 1942, she and her sister, also a convert, were pushed like cattle into a train truck moving East. They were never heard of again. They were only two, of untold millions, whose anonymous mass slaughter will make the poor twentieth century, for all its wonderful scientific and humanitarian achievement, infamous among the centuries of history.

Though never heard of on earth again, Sister Benedicta's life, because of her faith in God, is one of those which shines amid the darkness of that dreadful decade and points to some mysterious meaning in the pyres of corpses. In 1939, six months before Hitler's insane march into Poland, Edith Stein had offered her life to Our Lord 'as a sacrificial expiation for the sake of true peace: that the Antichrist's sway may be broken, if possible, without another world war, and that a new order may be established'. 'I am doing this today,' she said, 'because it is already the twelfth hour.'

The power of the Cross has been demonstrated by her influence since her death. Former SS men and concentration camp authorities testified that the example and influence of Edith Stein have brought them to remorse and repentance and that her prayers forced them, almost against their will, to faith and expiation. Edith Stein, through her identification with Christ on the Cross, has become a power for reconciliation between hating people and for return for faithless people to God.

It is only in Christ and through His Cross that fallen, sinful humans can ever have peace with God or with one another. Christ came as Prince of Peace offering peace on earth to all who would have the goodwill to accept His law of love. But the Prince of Peace Himself died a death of atrocious cruelty and injustice, a victim of the violence He came to banish from the earth.

He hung on the Cross, battered and insulted, bruised and bleeding, until violence could do no more to Him, until there was no more nerve to torture, no more blood to shed. He was the vicarious victim of all the hate and violence of the world, the representative of every persecuted Jew or displaced person or despised individual or group. When death came, they were surprised that it came so soon. 'They usually last out longer, these types.' As He hung there dead, peace and the hope of peace seemed to have died with Him. Three days later, His friends could speak of Him only as a great 'might-have-been'. 'Our hope had been that He would have been the one to set Israel free.' But now it was all over – another pipe dream smashed by the jack-boot of history.

But they were wrong. That morning a grave had opened, a dead man rose, the defeated had triumphed. Christ had risen. He was now free for ever from defeat and death, from sin and hate and evil. The tortured body had become the pledge of peace and the bond of love.

The achievement of peace, either at social, national or international level, is an intimidating task. It calls for faith, charity, hope, prayer, and also for technical skill, social development, economic planning, and diplomatic science. It calls for faith put energetically to work through love.

Clement of Alexandria, in the second century, wrote:

> Now the trumpet sounds with a mighty voice,
> calling the soldiers of the world to arms, announcing war;

> And shall not Christ, who has uttered His summons
> to peace even to the ends of the earth,
> Summon together His own soldiers of peace?
> Indeed He has called to arms with His blood and
> His word an army that sheds no blood …
> Let us be armed for peace, putting on the armour of
> justice,
> Seizing the shield of faith …

The message is the same as that of Edith Stein. The world can be saved and peace restored only through the power of the Cross of Christ. That Christ, raised upon the Cross, is raised up again at the Elevation of our Mass. All who believe in Him lifted up will be drawn by Him to the oneness and peace of the Father. There is no other name under heaven given to us whereby we can be saved. He is our peace.

'Peace Through Tolerance', World Day of Peace Address, 1 January 1988, St Anne's Catholic Church, Belfast

Having been bishop of Ardagh and Clonmacnois for fifteen years, Cahal Daly was appointed bishop of Down and Connor on 8 September 1982. At his installation homily he stated that 'to end violence in a just and reconciled society is our most urgent task'. He acknowledged the 'sad lack of trustfulness' between the divided communities and the need for 'each community to be ready to accept the other as the other sees and knows itself'. The following address reflects Bishop Daly's experience in his first five years in Down and Connor.

There are few places where the need to pray and to work for peace is more urgent than it is in our own country. Prayer for peace in all the Churches has been continuous. Efforts for peace and mutual understanding between our divided communities have been perseveringly pursued by clergy and laity in all the main Christian Communions. Addresses, appeals and exhortations for peace have been countless. Political initiatives have been courageously undertaken, which brought hope to some, but met with rejection from others. Great surges of intense desire for peace and reconciliation have swept across the whole country but have often ebbed away again like receding waves, leaving the shore as bleak and forbidding as before.

Some give in to the temptation of despair, or at least of fatalistic acceptance of the inevitability of continuing violence. Some opt out; seeing no future in this country, they emigrate, leaving the whole of society poorer for their going. Some opt out internally; losing interest in our problems and despairing of all possibility of their solution; they get on with their own individual and professional lives. This is particularly the temptation for those who live in more comfortable conditions and surroundings, insulated physically and psychologically from the areas where violence is endemic and from the problems of the people who live there.

What is the Christian response? Is there a Christian response? Is the Gospel message relevant to our situation? Is the Church just a helpless observer of events which it cannot control or even influence, or can the Church play an effective part in the making of peace? Pope John Paul said to his brothers and sisters in the faith:

> The commitment to peace is one of the testimonies which today makes us credible in the eyes of the world, and especially in the eyes of the younger generation. The great challenge facing [humanity] ... is found in the Gospel Beatitude: 'Blessed are the peacemakers' (Mt 5:9).

He pointed out that religious beliefs are still penalised in various parts of the world, sometimes by what he called 'subtle forms of discrimination aimed at believers and communities'. 'This state of affairs, in itself intolerable, is also a bad omen for peace.'

Sectarianism, which has for generations plagued our society, is still a major source of our afflictions. Sectarian murders and attempted murders have kept whole communities in terror. The elimination of sectarianism, in personal and community attitudes and in inter-community relationships and practices, must be a matter of grave concern for all the Churches and for all Christians. Theological dialogue, taking account of any features special to the religious traditions in Northern Ireland, could help towards better mutual understanding of the genuine beliefs of others, and could help to dispel inherited and unexamined stereotypes. Contacts at local level between clergy and laity of different denominations must become regular features of Church life, and not just be reserved for special occasions. It is precisely by their commitment to peace and to peaceful coexistence that every religious community and every individual believer can test the genuineness of their commitment to solidarity with their brothers and sisters.

Justice, Truth and Peace

There is an intrinsic connection between the demands of justice, truth and peace. A basic requirement for movement towards peace in our society is a recognition of the truth, an acceptance of the reality, of the politically divided society, the communities without political consensus, that we in Northern Ireland are. Spokespersons from the extreme wings of both communities persist in refusing to face this truth or to accept this reality. Loyalists still speak of 'the Ulster people', when they clearly mean only the unionist part of the population. They are evading reality. They are running away from the truth. Republicans speak of the 'right of the Irish people to national self-determination, freedom and independence'. They are clearly referring only to the republican and nationalist part of the population. They are substituting rhetoric for truth; they are refusing to face reality. The reality is that hundreds of thousands of 'the Irish people' are and wish to remain British. They have an historic and moral right so to choose and so to remain. The reality is that hundreds of thousands of 'the Ulster people' are and wish to remain Irish. They have an historic and moral right so to choose and so to remain.

The traditional unionist principle was that of an exclusively 'internal' United Kingdom solution with 'no interference by a foreign power'. This is simply not true to the reality which is Northern Ireland. The traditional nationalist solution was a united Ireland, with unionists joining 'the rest of the Irish people' and 'no British presence'. This is equally false to the facts.

The real 'British presence' in this country is the hundreds of thousands of people who live here, who belong here, and who would still be a British presence in Ireland if the

British administration were to withdraw next week. Irish Government involvement is simply a recognition of the reality of the Irishness of the hundreds of thousands of citizens of this State, whose nationality, whose allegiance, whose culture and whose identity is Irish. Irish Government involvement is not 'foreign interference'; it is simply an institutional statement of the internal reality which makes up Northern Ireland. Both the nationalist and the unionist traditions, both the Irish and the British identities, in this country are historically and morally equally legitimate. No constitutional or institutional arrangements for Northern Ireland could be morally justified, or could effectively operate, which failed to do justice to both traditions and failed to give institutional expression to both cultures and both identities.

History has demonstrated that nationalists cannot be coerced into a univocally British and unionist State and cannot be peacefully governed in it without their consent. History has equally demonstrated that unionists cannot be coerced into a nationalist Ireland and could not be peacefully governed in it without their consent.

There is no way that either community can attain its own cherished political objectives other than through dialogue with the political representatives of the other community. Unionism aspires to a united Northern Ireland within the United Kingdom. There is no way that it can attain this aim other than through persuasion of nationalists to consent to it, and through the elaboration, in dialogue with nationalists, of political arrangements and institutions acceptable also to nationalists. No constitutional guarantees, no repetition of slogans, will substitute for this. Unionism can succeed and survive only through demonstrating its own inherent capacity for persuasion through dialogue, and through proving its readiness for fairness and justice to its fellow citizens, under institutions acceptable to both communities in Northern Ireland. Nationalism aspires to a united island of Ireland. There is no way that it can attain this aim, other than through persuasion of unionists to consent to this, and through the elaboration, in dialogue with unionists, of political arrangements and institutions acceptable also to unionists. Nationalism can succeed only by persuasion through dialogue and through its readiness to respect and accommodate the British identity and United Kingdom allegiance of unionists, under institutions acceptable to both communities.

The Christian Response

I asked earlier what is the Christian response to our situation? It might seem that I have given a political answer to a religious question. But religion has to do with life, with all of life, including life in society; it has to do with relationships between individuals and groups and communities in society; it has to do with the structures and institutions which shape relationships between groups and communities in society. It has to do with personal and community rights, with inter-personal and inter-community justice and social justice. It has to do with political truth and integrity. It has to do with peace and with justice and truth, which are the requirements of peace. What I have been speaking about is the intrinsic connection between the demands of justice, truth and peace. These are all Christian virtues. Few words are more frequently found in the Bible than the words justice, truth and peace.

But in Christ all these terms are raised to a new level of reality and given a new depth of meaning. They are each of them shown by Christ to be applications of one single commandment, His new commandment of love. Christ's teaching about love is so new a concept that a new name had to be found for it in New Testament Greek. The older term for love, *eros*, had a self-gratifying, self-seeking note to it. The new term, *agape*, means unselfish, un-self-seeking, un-self-interested love. It is in fact a sharing by us in the love of God; indeed, it is our sharing through Christ in the very life of God, since God is love. Christ calls it a new commandment, in spite of the fact that love is a constant theme throughout the Old Testament. The commandment of love of God and love of neighbour was the great commandment of God to which Israel was bidden to listen every day and many times a day. How then is Christ's commandment new?

Christ's commandment of love is new because, like God's love for us, it always makes the first move. It always takes the initiative. It goes out to the unloved and the unlovable and makes them lovable and loved by first loving them as they are. God's love does not wait until we are His friends. It is His love which makes us His friends. St Paul says that God loved us and reconciled us with Himself through His Son 'while we were still enemies' (cf. Rm 5:10). God's love does not wait for our response: our response is the result of His love for us; our love for Him and for others is the gift of His love to us. God's love does not even wait for us to change and to repent before He forgives us; we are able to change and able to repent because He has already forgiven us in Christ. Our repentance is simply our acceptance of the forgiveness which He offers us; it is our accepting the reconciliation He has already brought about for us through Christ. We never love God first; He always loves us first, and our love for God and for others is simply our loving and thank-filled recognition that we are loved by Him.

Political Love

Our love for God and for others must determine all our attitudes, our emotions, our judgements, our relationships in our individual and family and professional lives, but also in our communal and political lives. Love must inform our politics as well as our personal behaviour if we are to be truly Christian. Love is the first political imperative for the Christian.

To be genuinely Christian, this love must be always first to take initiatives, ready to take risks, prepared for rebuff and refusal. In unforgettable terms, St Paul describes Christian love as:

> always patient and kind. ... never rude or selfish; it does not take offence and is not resentful ...; it is always ready to excuse, to trust, to hope and to endure whatever comes. (1 Cor 13:4-7)

How radically our situation would be transformed in Northern Ireland if we really applied the norm of Christian love to our political behaviour. The Christian cannot wait, for 'the others' can be changed only by our loving them first as they are. The Christian cannot lay down conditions for loving or make exceptions or exclude certain groups or communities. We must love our enemies, even while they are still hostile. The Lord's words are quite categorical; there is no place to hide from His challenge:

> I say this to you: love your enemies and pray for those who persecute you. In this way, you will be sons and daughters of your Father in heaven, for He causes His sun to rise on the bad as well as the on the good. ...

> If you love those who love you, what right have you to claim any credit? ... If you save your greetings for your brothers and sisters, are you doing anything exceptional? Even the pagans do as much, do they not? You must therefore be perfect, just as your heavenly Father is perfect. (Mt 5:44-8)

The Christian Revolution

I am afraid that we Christians have often 'domesticated' and 'tamed' and 'privatised' and diluted these words, as we have done with other words from the lips of Christ. We have called them 'counsels of perfection', thereby subtly satisfying ourselves that they are meant for exceptional 'elite' groups in the Church, but not for 'ordinary Christians' like ourselves. But Christ is here stating basic elementary Christian precepts, meant for all Christians. They are the actual identification marks of the followers of Christ. Christ said:

> By this love you have for one another everyone will know that you are My disciples. (Jn 13:35)

We must try to realise again how radical, how revolutionary Christianity is. We must see afresh what a radical transformation it has to make in our lives, what a revolution it is meant to create in our society. The Christian, every Christian, is called to be a revolutionary, but a revolutionary of love. For ourselves and for our society, it is nothing less than a 'new creation', a new social order, a 'new heaven and a new earth'. It means a death to old or 'ordinary' ways of thinking and behaving and rising to a new life in Christ. It means putting on 'the new self, that has been created in God's way' (cf. Eph 4:24). It means having in us 'the same mind that was also in Christ Jesus' (cf. Phil 2:5). St Paul says quite firmly:

> I urge you in the name of the Lord not to go on living the aimless kind of life that pagans live. ... That is not the way you have learnt from Christ, unless you failed to hear Him properly when you were taught what the truth is in Jesus. You must give up your old way of life; you must put aside your old self. ... Your mind must be renewed by a spiritual revolution. (Eph 4:17, 20-3)

Let us never suppose that God's Kingdom of justice, love and peace exists only outside of time and space beyond history. It is true that the full manifestation and actualisation of the Kingdom take place at Christ's Second Coming. But the Kingdom is also already here. It is a reality in our world. It is the mightiest power in our society and in our world. The Kingdom is very near to us. It is in the midst of us (cf. Lk 17:21). The Kingdom is Christ in us, Christ amongst us, Christ in all the death-defeating power of His love, in the victory and glory of His resurrection. In Christ, love has triumphed. No hate can finally prevail against it. God's love has the first word in creation and in salvation. Love, through Him, will have the last word in human history.

'From the Justice of Each Comes Peace for All', World Day of Peace Address, 1 January 1998, Corpus Christi Church, Drumcondra

Cardinal Daly retired on 1 October 1996. In this, his final address for World Day of Peace, given less than five months before the signing of the Good Friday Agreement, he includes some reflections on the continuing violence in Northern Ireland, which he sees as weakening the moral influence of Ireland on broader issues of justice such as poverty in the world's least developed countries, international debt and the arms trade. He praises the persistent work of the British and Irish governments and the engagement of the United States administration in seeking peace.

He refers to two murders. The first was the murder on 27 December 1997 of Billy Wright, aged thirty-seven. Mr Wright, who was a leader of the Loyalist Volunteer Force (LVF), was serving a prison sentence in the Maze prison. He was sitting in a prison van awaiting transport to the LVF visiting area of the prison when he was shot dead by INLA prisoners. The second murder was that of Seamus Dillon, aged forty-six, who was working as a doorman at a Dungannon hotel on the night of the murder of Billy Wright. He was shot dead in what was believed to be a LVF reprisal attack for the murder of Mr Wright.

Not unnaturally, the Cardinal did not seek in his final address to evaluate the impact of his own work for peace. It has been left to others, including two of the leading negotiators of the Good Friday Agreement, Tony Blair, former British prime minister, and Bertie Ahern, former Irish taoiseach, to do so. Mr Ahern described him as a beacon in the wilderness of community polarisation and senseless violence. 'He stood for calm, for reasoned debate, for equity and justice, and raised his voice above the tumult to speak of moral rights, of the common Christian bonds which in religion unite so many of our communities.' Mr Blair referred to him as a 'real and lasting example of effective religious leadership working to build peace and resolve conflict by breaking down barriers between communities'.

The UN's Universal Declaration of Human Rights, which was adopted on 10 December 1948, states in its Preamble:

> Recognition of the inherent dignity and equality and the inalienable rights of all members of the human family is the foundation of freedom and justice and peace in the world.

Universality and indivisibility are therefore inherent in the very meaning of human rights. Solidarity is without frontiers. Poorer nations too have the right to have access to a fair and just share in the benefits of the global market.

The share of the world's wealth which poorer countries actually do have can be illustrated by a few figures. The wealth of the world's ten richest billionaires is one-and-a-half times greater than the aggregate annual national income of forty-nine of the world's least developed countries. A worker in a toy factory in Indonesia which produces toys for Disney earns 17 pence per hour; Disney's Chief Executive earns £6,700 per hour. Over the past thirty years, the income of the wealthiest people in the world has doubled in relation to the income of the poorest. In 1960, the wealthiest 20% earned thirty times more than the poorest 20%; in 1997, they earned sixty times more. The gap between rich and poor at world level is enormous, and it is widening by the year. The poor countries of the world are becoming poorer at the same time as the wealthy nations become richer.

The Debt Burden

One of the causes of the accelerating pauperisation of the poorer nations is the heavy burden of external debt which they carry, a burden which is heaviest in the countries of Sub-

Saharan Africa, South and East Asia and some countries in Latin America. A few figures will graphically illustrate the effects of this debt.

The aggregate national debt owed by the under-developed world to the developed world is such that each individual in the poorer countries owes £250 to the richer countries; and this for many is more than one full year's wages. Each year the underdeveloped world pays the West three times more in debt repayments than it receives from the West in aid. Africa has to spend four times as much on debt repayment as it spends on health care. The Council for Justice and Peace warns about the consequences of this situation for world peace; it speaks of 'dangerous and costly international insecurity'. The Pope has asked Christians to raise their voices on behalf of all the poor of the world, and to use their influence to urge reduction or cancellation of the international debt which seriously threatens the future of many nations. Financial institutions, banks and multinational corporations have an important role and responsibility in this process; they cannot morally demand contract fulfilment, by any and all means, especially if the debtor is in a situation of extreme need.

Admittedly, in many poor countries, borrowed money has been misappropriated by corruption or misapplied by despotic regimes for the purchase of weapons for the repression of their citizens or the prosecution of civil wars. But a new beginning in these countries is possible only when education is improved, employment increased and poverty reduced; and these developments in turn become possible only when the debt burden is lifted.

The Arms Trade

A major source of poverty and hardship in the world and

a major cause of the widening gap between rich and poor nations is the incidence across the world of wars and civil or tribal conflicts and of terrorism. This in turn is made possible by the arms trade. We know to our own cost in Ireland the havoc and the misery which are wrought as a result of the transhipment of weapons; and the weapons illegally imported into Ireland are only a fraction of those legally sold abroad, and more often sold by the wealthy nations to the poorer ones. Once more, some figures give an indication of the material extent and the moral enormity of the problem.

The time since the end of World War II might be seen in history as a period of comparative world peace; yet, more than three million people have been killed in war over that period, and there are fifteen million refugees, mostly driven from their homes by wars. The Pontifical Council for Justice and Peace in 1994 declared: 'Never before has our earth known so many armed conflicts, fed by a proliferation of arms, which is often taken for granted.' All this is fuelled by the trade in weapons. Arms imports are directly linked to poverty and to military repression. Arms exports are characteristic of the 'First World', namely the richer nations. The trade is worth nearly one thousand billion dollars to rich countries. Nearly half a million of the world's scientists are involved in military-related research projects. The United States heads the list of arms exporting countries; Britain comes second. Ten years ago, Britain was exporting five billion dollars' worth of military equipment to governments overseas, three-fourths of these being in poorer countries in the underdeveloped world. This included 150 million dollars' worth of weaponry sold to Indonesia, some of it undoubtedly used for military repression of the people of East Timor.

Comparative figures show how much the expectation of life and the quality of life in poorer countries could be bettered if the priorities of both the exporting and the importing countries were changed. It costs twenty-one thousand dollars to keep a B1 bomber in the air for one hour. This amount alone could set up maternal health units in ten African villages. One intercontinental Stealth Bomber, or one Seawolf nuclear high-powered submarine, each costing some two-and-a-half billion dollars, would be enough to provide immunisation vaccines for all the children of the underdeveloped world and would save many hundreds of thousands of young lives. In some poorer countries, military expenditure exceeds the total expenditure on education and health combined.

Such figures show that the problems of poverty and hunger and disease could be resolved if there were the political will to do so. It is sad to reflect that few individuals in the so called 'Great Power' nations question taxation for military purposes; but there is no political pressure for taxation to relieve poverty. One United States commentator remarked, 'Governments are armed to destroy everything except poverty.' The truth is that the purchase and the use of arms by poor countries create greater poverty.

Moral Influence

I know that the questions of international debt and the arms trade are complex ones, and that they may seem remote from us in this country and beyond our power to influence. Nevertheless, the Republic of Ireland has a significant international image and an undoubted international prestige. Irish missionaries are found all over the underdeveloped world. Trócaire and Concern and similar Irish aid and development organisations are known and respected across that world. Many Irish men and women have been directly exposed to ethnic or tribal wars in such countries as Somalia, the Sudan and Rwanda. Irish Army and Garda peace personnel are known and respected in the councils of the United Nations and of Europe. Our own Mary Robinson is UN Commissioner for Human Rights. This country's experience of famine enables us to have unique empathy with today's famine victims across the world. We could exert considerable moral influence in areas like world poverty, world debt and the arms trade. We could make a significant contribution in helping to change that lack of political commitment, which, according to the 1997 UN Development Report, is 'the real obstacle to poverty eradication'. 'Extreme poverty', according to that report, 'can be banished from the globe by early next century', if the political commitment to do so were there.

This country's rich spiritual tradition gives us unique resources for the task of responding to the growing crisis of world poverty and injustice. Europe's great economic and technical might needs what [philosopher Henri] Bergson called 'a supplement of soul'. Ireland is better placed than most European countries to offer that supplement of soul.

Peace in Northern Ireland

Our moral influence in these areas is, of course, weakened by the continuing conflict in Northern Ireland. It would be greatly enhanced by the achievement of peace through negotiation and by agreement in that distressful part of the island. Successive Irish governments, their ministers and their officials, over the past quarter-century, have devoted much energy and patience and great skill to finding solutions to the conflict there. So, too, have successive

British administrations. Very notable help has also been received from the United States. It seems to me a great pity that the efforts of the respective governments and specifically of the Irish Government have been viewed with suspicion, particularly by the unionist community. It is regrettable that the Irish Government's efforts are not seen by unionists as disinterestedly designed to secure peace and stability for the benefit of unionists as well as that of nationalists, a peace commanding unionist consent as well as nationalist consent, a peace guaranteeing unionist rights as well as nationalist rights.

It has also been unfortunate that both republicans and unionists have seen the conflict as being caused or as being perpetuated by outside or foreign interference in the internal affairs of Northern Ireland or of Ireland, respectively. For republicans, the foreign body is Britain; for unionists, the foreign body is the Irish Government. This mindset has inhibited both communities from seeing that the real problems are internal to Northern Ireland, but that, at the same time, the Northern Ireland communities are unable to resolve their internal problems on their own. This is not simply due to perversity. It is due to the respective self-identification of each community; the unionists seeing their identity and their future in alignment with Britain, the republicans, and indeed the wider nationalist community, seeing theirs in alignment with the rest of Ireland. The involvement of both governments is, therefore, an internal requirement of the situation which is Northern Ireland; it is an internal component of the reality which is Northern Ireland. Sheer political realism, and enlightened political self-interest, require from both Northern Ireland communities cooperation with the two governments, as well as inclusive dialogue with one another, in the search for a settlement, which has to be agreed by both governments and by both communities, but which will immeasurably benefit both communities.

Meanwhile, we have all been shocked by the disastrous slaying of Billy Wright in the Maze Prison and the killing of Seamus Dillon at the Glengannon Hotel near Dungannon, in what was obviously intended as a random and potentially multiple sectarian assassination attempt. These killings demonstrate once more the stark truth, which should have been obvious from the very beginning, namely, that any recourse to armed violence by either side in Northern Ireland had inevitably to be seen as sectarian, and would become in fact sectarian, no matter what the original intention might have been. If the bloodshed of the past years has taught any lesson, it is that violence can be no part of any resolution of the problems of Northern Ireland.

PART 2: *SPECIFIC CHALLENGES TO PEACE*

There were many occasions when, as bishop or cardinal, Cahal Daly spoke about particular challenges to the peace process. The following are some examples of those challenges.

The Birmingham Six

On 6 February 1988 Bishop Daly returned from a visit to two of the Birmingham Six in Wormwood Scrubs prison and made the following statement.

After thirteen years in prison and a long campaign conducted on their behalf by a most dedicated body of journalists, solicitors, barristers, Members of Parliament and clergy, hopes of the release of the Birmingham Six had been raised and then bitterly dashed. It was not only the verdict of the Court of Appeal which caused dismay. It was also the total and seemingly almost contemptuous rejection of every part of the case argued for the men by their able Counsel. It was also the cold, insensitive and unfeeling way in which the verdict was felt to be delivered. Even learned Judges should remember that they are only weak, human and fallible instruments of justice; they are not arbiters of final judgement.

I spent three days in the courtroom at the Old Bailey while the Appeal Court hearing was in progress. I have spoken with many persons whose opinion I hold in high regard and who know the Birmingham Six intimately over all the years of their imprisonment. From these conversations and from my own meetings with the men, I am convinced of the innocence of the Birmingham Six. I believe that it was their misfortune to be in the wrong place at the wrong time and to be caught in a maze of circumstances which, at that particular time, and given the mood which understandably swept through Britain in the wake of the appalling carnage of Birmingham, looked suspicious and were susceptible of a sinister interpretation, but which were innocent and were all of them capable of a perfectly innocuous interpretation. The men were caught in a web of Kafkaesque concatenations of circumstances, whose every single element had a perfectly innocent explanation, but all of which together carried by association and convergence an appearance of guilt.

On 4 February 1988 the influential and internationally respected British journal *The Economist* stated:

> Respectable bishops, parliamentarians (British and Irish) and journalists have been crying that justice miscarried. To placate them the Home Secretary last year asked the Court of Appeal to consider three options: to order the convicts released; to call a fresh trial; or to let the sentences stand. It let them stand. The men had been tortured. As the Lord Chief Justice of England said: 'There was no doubt they had been violently assaulted in the prison by prison officers and/or prisoners.' But the prison officers charged with injuring them were acquitted ... It was to the police that they made their confused confessions ... The Birmingham trial underlines the need to scrap the peculiar willingness of English courts to accept uncorroborated confessions, which openly invite police abuse.

This case should not be made the occasion of mere British-bashing. After all, it is people in Britain – people of integrity in the legal profession and many journalists and some Members of Parliament who have been the main protagonists of the cause of the Six.

A major share of the responsibility for the imprisonment of the Six rests here in Ireland. The IRA know who prepared and planted the Birmingham bombs. The people who were involved in the outrage and leaders of their organisation carry guilt for the suffering of the Birmingham Six. They could even now secure their vindication and their release.

Murders of Members of the Security Forces

Peter Nesbitt, who was a single man aged thirty-two years, was a draughtsman at Shorts aircraft factory in Belfast and a reserve RUC police officer. He was killed by an IRA booby trap bomb on the junction of Woodville Road and Crumlin Road in North Belfast when responding to a hoax call about a robbery in a sweet shop. On 13 March 1987, just before the funeral of Mr Nesbitt, police received reports that a bomb had been left in the vicinity of Roselawn Cemetery, Belfast. Two of the RUC officers who responded to the reports were injured when a car bomb planted by the IRA exploded.

Evil has manifested itself in the murder on 10 March 1987 of Reserve Constable Nesbitt who was responding promptly and efficiently to what purported to be a genuine call for police help but was a lure into a murder trap. Evil has shown a new and horrifying face in a murder attempt at the very gates of a cemetery, timed on the occasion of the funeral of the constable and adding a new dimension of anguish to the heartbreak of his relatives.

Such deeds must be abhorred absolutely and condemned unconditionally by both communities. Such deeds are a massive obstacle to any hope of normal policing in areas afflicted and persecuted by criminal elements.

In the presence of the coffin of another victim one reflects that many Protestant homes in Northern Ireland and many homes in Britain have witnessed similar scenes of grief. Many Irish Protestant wives have been left heart-broken and many children orphaned through the murder of their loved ones serving in the RUC or the UDR. Many homes of servicemen in Britain have been similarly devastated. Those who planned and perpetrated these murders cannot claim any justification for their actions. It cannot be too frequently or too firmly repeated that there are no legitimate targets. There is no moral justification for any politically motivated killing in the Northern Ireland situation. There is no political cause that can be advanced through violence and no community which can be helped or protected by paramilitary violence.

The Canary Wharf Bombing, 9 February 1996

On 31 August 1994 the IRA announced a ceasefire, and on 13 October 1994 the Combined Loyalist Military Command announced a truce which would be linked to the IRA ceasefire. The IRA issued a statement on 9 February 1996 revoking the ceasefire with effect from 6 p.m. that day. At around 6.30 p.m., following warning calls that a large bomb had been placed at South Quay Station, Marsh Wall, Canary Wharf, London, a Ford flat-backed lorry was identified as a suspect vehicle. While the area was being evacuated, the vehicle exploded. Two people were killed and more than a hundred were injured. The next ceasefire announced by the IRA was on 20 July 1997.

The London bomb outrage at Canary Wharf and the accompanying statement by the IRA saying that their ceasefire is over constitute the bleakest message which has been delivered to the people of this country for a long time.

I wish first of all to state my absolute and unqualified condemnation of the London outrage. It was morally evil and gravely sinful. I offer my sincere sympathy to the relatives of the dead and to all the people injured and shocked by this evil deed. I wish to repeat what I have so often said before that there is not any moral justification for the use of physical force. Having enjoyed seventeen months' respite from violence, people have had the opportunity to reflect on its nature and its consequences, and to see both how morally wrong it is and how politically futile it is. The possibility of a full-scale resumption of violence fills people with dread.

Many feel that the pace of the peace process has been too slow and that precious opportunities for political progress through talks have been recklessly thrown away. Others feel that any change to the political structures in Northern Ireland would be to the detriment and disadvantage of their community. There will be an urge to blame others and to say, 'it was their fault'. Others again will greet the breakdown of the ceasefire with a chorus of self-indulgent cries of 'I told you so'.

We should try to avoid facile reactions. Instead of swopping recriminations and blaming 'the others' we should humbly and honestly ask ourselves how much we, each of us, failed to do or to say what might have helped the cause of peace, and whether things we did or said hindered the cause of peace. May God give us now the will and the means to save the peace process in spite of what has happened.

Garvaghy Road March from Drumcree Parish Church, 12 July 1996

The summer of 1996 saw very significant civil unrest in Northern Ireland. A particular challenging area was the mainly nationalist Garvaghy Road, Portadown. The police banned a Drumcree Orange parade from marching along that road from Drumcree Church but the Orangemen responded that they would march nonetheless. There was rioting and the erection of road blocks in many parts of Northern Ireland and the police reversed the ban and allowed the march to go ahead on 12 July.

The memorial referred to by Cardinal Daly below was erected in memory of eight Protestant workmen from the Ballymena-based firm Karl Construction who were killed by an IRA explosive device at the Teebane Crossroads as they were returning from their work at an army base on 17 January 1992.

Today has been a dark day in the history of Northern Ireland. The decision to force through the Orange parade along the Garvaghy Road in Portadown in defiance of the feelings of the residents was a bad decision, a mistaken decision, a disastrous decision. The consequences for confidence in the rule of law can be calamitous. The State has been seen to capitulate before lawless violence and the threat of violence. I cannot see how the decision can be justified on security grounds or on grounds of balance of security risks.

There is a widespread feeling in nationalist circles in Portadown that the Garvaghy Road residents were 'set up'. They feel betrayed and it would be hard for them to feel otherwise. We Church leaders worked without ceasing through two days and nights to seek a solution to the Drumcree march impasse. The Garvaghy Road residents have painful memories of having last year made a generous concession in the interest of peace, only to find their concession greeted with displays of Orange and unionist triumphalism. They tried very hard over the following twelve months to find a reasonable solution for this year's march through dialogue and by agreement with the Orange Order. Their repeated requests for meetings and dialogue were spurned.

I understand their feelings of betrayal; indeed I personally share their feelings. Today I joined with other Church leaders in seeking to have dialogue with representatives of both communities separately. The efforts failed. The meetings ended without any real dialogue having been engaged. We accepted that for the moment we had not succeeded but we drafted a statement indicating that we continued to hope for and to work for a just and fair agreement between both sides. Our statement was completed and was issued before the Chief Constable announced his decision [to reverse his earlier decision of 6 July 1996 to re-route the march away from Garvaghy Road and] to allow the march down the Garvaghy Road.

I was shocked and dismayed by the decision. I could not believe what I was hearing. The decision leaves the future very bleak and uncertain. There is great anger throughout the whole nationalist community across Northern Ireland. There is great pain. There is great fear. For me, the events of today and of the days of the Drumcree 'stand-off' reveal in stark form the deep-seated injustices which still mark our society. They manifest the ugly sectarianism which persists in this society and which is an affront to our Christian professions.

It is said that the police authorities simply could not hold the line against overwhelming numbers of Orangemen. But surely the authorities of the State have the responsibility to protect its citizens in all circumstances and in face of all threats from other citizens. Are there not powers at the disposal of the police and government to avert assemblies for an illegal purpose? Can the police not control the public thoroughfares? There were days leading to the Twelfth of July when preventive action could have been taken if the will to do so had been there. Many nationalists are asking whether the RUC would have allowed a comparable number of nationalists to assemble with the clear intention of overwhelming the police by force of superior numbers. Are there two systems of law in operation in this land? Or are we to assume that there are circumstances in which the rule of law simply cannot be enforced by the forces of law and order in Northern Ireland?

We pray at this time for all those who have been injured in clashes with the police. Several are in hospital. One has already died. Others are critically ill. Seeing the mutilated young men and their distraught parents has brought home to me the sheer awfulness and evil of all violence.

I do not forget, and I hope none of us forget, that policemen have been injured and traumatised. Police men and women have distraught parents too, and spouses and children. Let us pray for them too. The Chief Constable and the police should not have been left to accept the responsibility for a decision which was clearly taken for political reasons and to bear the consequences of an abdication of responsibility by the British Government.

There is however now a huge crisis of confidence in the police among the nationalist community at large. In my own modest way I have tried for years to urge both the police and the Catholic public to work to build up mutual trust and confidence. Restoration of confidence will require immense and prolonged efforts on the part of the RUC and those efforts must be vigorously undertaken in a genuine spirit of humility, regret for what has happened and readiness for real change. Northern Ireland needs a police service in whose integrity and impartiality all political communities and all social strata can have confidence.

We have sadly seen some of the consequences of the decision to force the march through. I totally condemn all recourse to violence, all rioting, all throwing of stones or, even worse, of petrol bombs. I condemn all blocking of roads, all interference with the rights of citizens to a peaceful and orderly way of life.

I deplore the destruction of the memorial to the Protestants murdered by the IRA at Teebane. Surely at least the dead should be allowed to rest in peace. Surely the relatives have suffered enough without this. Catholics who have known similar suffering will extend their sincere sympathy to the bereaved of the Teebane massacre.

The peaceful pursuit of justice must be intensified in spite of, and indeed because of, the Garvaghy Road decision. The peace process with all that it promised all of us for a better future must not be destroyed in the heat of the understandable passions aroused by that decision.

I call for intense prayer on the part of all our people, that reason and peace and Christian love and forbearance may prevail. Let us all commend ourselves to the loving mercy of God.

Canon Edward O'Donnell, now parish priest of St Brigid's, Belfast, and an ecumenical canon of St Anne's Church of Ireland Cathedral, Belfast, was secretary to Cahal Daly when he was bishop of Down and Connor. He said that Cardinal Daly 'did not underestimate the problems facing the Church, nor did he believe that there were simple solutions around the corner. But he was convinced that the credibility of the Church could only come from Christ. He was acutely aware of the importance of translating Christ's gospel into pastoral initiatives, geared to a land in which the concept of "Christian society" is now seriously weakened and in some places gone.'

Louis McRedmond, former RTÉ head of information, referred to Cahal Daly's ministry as 'flying in the face of cherished resentments. It was not an upbraiding of his own; it was, rather, showing them and their Protestant neighbours alike how Christians should react in the troubled times they lived through. Peace was to be found in repudiating recrimination.'

CHAPTER 3

A Civilisation of Love

God's Love for Us

In his homily in St Patrick's Cathedral, Armagh, on 16 December 1990, when he was being installed as archbishop, Cahal Daly said that no words recur more often in the New Testament than 'love' and 'joy' and that the Church's whole message is therefore a message of love – of God's incredible love for us and Christ's new commandment that we love one another as he has loved us. The importance of love in all its manifestations in human life was a recurring theme in his preaching.

God makes Himself known to us as the One who loves us; He loves us more than we can ever imagine; His very name is Love. The whole Bible, the greatest love story ever, tells of all the extraordinary things God has done out of love for us whom He calls His children. If we were ever to have doubts about God's love for us, we only need to look at the Cross and say, 'That scourge mark was for me; that nail was for me; that gash in His side was for me.' We are lovable because God makes us so by loving us and we love others because God has made them lovable.

Love in the Family

In 1985 the Irish bishops decided to issue a Lenten pastoral letter entitled 'Love is for Life'. Cahal Daly was charged with the task of writing the letter, from which some of the following extracts are taken.

In marriage love finds one of its most beautiful expressions; just to see a young bridal couple in love bright with the promise of lifelong happiness evokes joy in others. Joy is also evoked by seeing a husband and wife in the mature and settled happiness of their marriage, when they have 'grown into' one another's personalities to a point where each of them singly would be much less than half of what the two of them have become together.

It is God who joins a married couple together in the most intimate physical expressions of their love in bodily union which is a way of saying 'I love you. There is nobody else in all the world I love in the way I love you. I love you just for being you. I want to share my life and my world with you. I need you to love me and to love me not just now but always. I will never let you down or walk out on you. I will stay with you through thick and thin.' An act of sexual union which truly and honestly expresses total and life-long and exclusive union between a man and a woman is also an act which is open to new life in a child. Sexual union can express forgiveness, reconciliation, sorrow for selfishness, healing of hurts. It speaks of a couple's thankfulness for each other, their peaceful contentment with each other. It carries the promise of seeing life through together with each other.

Love in marriage does not just happen; it has to be worked at and worked at constantly, fostered, wanted and willed. It has stages for every phase and mood and changing lifestyle. Marriage needs to be a continuing courtship and it needs a lifetime for its full growth. The difficulties of adjustment to marriage, the annoyances which people cause to one another, the disappointments, the disagreements and disputes, the rows and the anger, these can sadly be for some a reason for withdrawing from one another into sullen silence or even into a kind of cold war. But disagreements can also bring a couple closer together in a more realistic way. This will happen, however, only if married people are ready to forgive and ask forgiveness, if they are both ready to aim at conversion and to work steadily at change and new beginning. When man and woman have lived through love in God's presence until death do them part, they will have attained the only kind of maturity which ultimately counts: maturity in Christ.

Unfortunately, people do behave in ways that conflict with the true meaning of human love. Nevertheless these people need pastoral care and must be approached, not with condemnation and rebuke, but with sensitivity and compassion. The pastoral aim of Jesus was always to lead the sinner, kindly and gently but firmly, away from the sinful situation and to the peace of union with God's will and plan.

Pope John Paul II once said he would love to 'knock on the door of every family, to greet each family with deep affection and to spend time in each home'. That is what I and every bishop would like to do, if it were possible, for each family in all the dioceses of Ireland.

We would wish to witness the greatest expression of the shared life of the wife and the husband in their children who are 'flesh of the flesh and bone of the bone' of them both. A child is the love of a man and a woman for each other smiling back at both of them, in a face which unites the very features of them both. It is a circle of love which unites parents with one another and with their children in their home which is the 'domestic Church'.

Husband and wife love one another around their child and surround their child with an atmosphere of love. Children need the life-long love of parents in order to reach their full maturity and achieve their full potential as human beings and as children of God. Children need love as much as they need food. A child deprived of love is stunted in its personal growth. Children also have a right that their parents love one another. Children first learn about God through experiencing love in the family and particularly between the father and the mother.

Children suffer from discord in the home. Violence inflicted by one spouse against another is not only an intolerable offence against one's partner in Christ; it is also an offence against the children and a violence done to them. Violence against women is the most common and the most despicable form of violence in the home. Priests must keep insisting on its evil and depraved character.

Sexuality is a noble and beautiful gift of God to human beings. It is wonderful, literally, 'wonder-filled', but also wounded. It can be tender and humanising; it can be capricious and brutal; it can express itself as rapture or it can express itself as rape. A most appalling problem is that of child sexual abuse which does occur in the home or in the extended family or involves friends of the family. It is particularly perverse when the abuser is a parent or step-parent. Child abuse by a priest is one of the greatest wounds inflicted by churchmen on the Church in our time and one of the greatest betrayals of Christ by those called to be his closest followers and friends. A climate of true Christian love and sound moral values, and a climate of faith and prayer in the home, must accompany all programmes of prevention of this odious abuse.

Love Between the Churches

A commitment to dialogue between the Christian churches was a hallmark of the life of Cahal Daly. His lifelong friendships with Christians of other denominations and the particular circumstances of Northern Ireland led to his conviction of the value and necessity of ecumenical engagement. He was involved in the first-ever Catholic–Protestant church meeting that took place in 1973 in Ballymascanlon, Co. Louth. Through his engagement in the subsequent regular Ballymascanlon meetings between the Christian churches, he succeeded in establishing excellent relations with leaders of other churches. Together with Rev. Dr Eric Gallagher, president of the Methodist Church in Ireland, he chaired the working party which produced in 1976 the seminal report Violence in Ireland: A Report to the Churches, *published by Veritas and Christian Journals Ltd. According to Dr Gallagher, that report had by 1980 led to more contact, more mutual respect and more understanding between the Churches than at any earlier period of Irish history. The book* Integration and Division: Geographical Perspectives on the Northern Ireland Problem *was published in 1997 by Academic Press.*

Ecumenism is not an 'optional extra' for Christians. It is the heart of our faith and an urgent imperative for the Churches in Northern Ireland. There are many examples of courageous and outstanding witness to the Gospel values of love and forgiveness, tolerance and peace among Christian communities here. I mention Fitzroy Presbyterian Church in Belfast as a synonym for these values, the very values by which Christ said that men and women would be recognised as disciples of his. I shared on at least three occasions in Services in that Church including with two Moderators and among my themes was that, as Christians gathered together to worship God in spirit and in truth, we know that it is only in Christ's saving Word that we shall find the way to true and lasting peace in our land.

Our common affirmation of faith will not ignore and cannot deny our doctrinal differences. But even here we must attempt to understand, not condemn. We must accept one another's good faith, rather than anathematise one another's doctrinal or moral beliefs as mere and deliberate aberrations. Deeper study will frequently show that differences can in part be seen as complementary rather than contradictory of our own beliefs. The either/or of controversy can often be tempered by the both/and of understanding. I am not calling for any facile assumption that doctrinal differences are unreal or unimportant. What I am saying is that differences can be viewed in a positive rather than just in a negative light. But this requires a deep understanding of our own faith and firm and enlightened fidelity to our own Church tradition. The more deeply one values and the more profoundly one enters into understanding of one's own Protestant or Catholic faith, the more fitted one is for ecumenical dialogue and the more convinced one is of the ecumenical obligations of the Christian.

There are some who would regard Northern Ireland as an ecumenical desert because, as Frederick W. Boal and J. Neville H. Douglas, in their book *Integration and Division: Geographical Perspectives on the Northern Ireland Problem,* remark, 'this strife . . . which has lasted since 1969 . . . is labelled as a conflict between Protestants and Roman Catholics and has been treated, in many instances, as a religious or holy war.' But these authors continue, 'Two points must be made at the outset – first that the Northern Ireland problem predates the existence of Northern Ireland as a political unit, and secondly, that the holy war interpretation is, at best, a vast over-simplification which enables its adherents to avoid any attempt at real understanding.'

The communities which were polarised by the conflict in Northern Ireland are differentiated by history, by culture, by sense of historical origin and sense of national identity, by political allegiance and aspiration, by contrasting experience of social and economic opportunity, by their respective sense of majority or minority status. At the same time the communities are differentiated by religious or denominational background and the other differences have historically been associated with denominational differences. This is what gives the conflict the appearance of a 'religious war'; which causes pain and even scandal to Christians everywhere.

While the Churches have each their specific share of blame and of guilt, they have also their individual and their common responsibilities and opportunities. Firstly, I submit that much mutual suspicion and prejudice is due to religious ignorance. This ignorance is two-fold. It is often ignorance of the teaching of our own Church, leading to a lack of full acceptance of the internal renewal in which each of our Churches has been engaged for some decades. There is also ignorance of, and therefore opposition to, the ecumenical movement. It is worth remarking that the modern ecumenical movement began in fact in the Protestant Churches; but the movement was entered into with enthusiasm by the Catholic Church particularly after the Vatican Council. There is still great need, however, for ecumenical education and for acceptance of ecumenism, not as a betrayal or a threat, but as an opportunity for new understanding of our own truth and for the enrichment of our own religious tradition through contact with others.

I believe that the attitude Jesus showed to each of the two types of community divisions which existed in his time and which impacted on virtually every inhabitant of the land has immediate relevance to our situation in this land of ours today. There was the division of Israelites themselves between Jews and Samaritans, and the division between all Israelites and the pagans, the *Goyim*, who were the Romans, Greeks, or others of non-Jewish race.

Jesus and the Samaritans

Cahal Daly wanted to emphasise the radical transformation effected by Jesus in his attitude to the Samaritans. The very term 'Samaritan' was once an expression of loathing but down through the Christian centuries, because of the teaching and example of Jesus, it has become a synonym for charity and goodness.

Let us look first at Jesus' attitude to the Samaritans. In the eyes of the Jews Samaritans were the people who had broken the unity of the United Kingdom of David and who had also departed from the religious unity centred on the Temple in Jerusalem, and who had consequently corrupted the true religion and the true worship of the Covenant community. Relations between the Samaritans and the Jews were at best relations of cold and suspicious separateness, and at worst open and sometime violent conflict. They lived in separate areas and rarely crossed into one another's territory. The tensions between the two communities became more marked at the time of their respective feasts; at such times, a Jew crossed at his peril into Samaria and vice versa.

These tensions often directly affected Jesus and his disciples. On one occasion, when they decided to risk passing through Samaria, a Samaritan village refused to allow them to pass through their village, because the Samaritans knew that they were on their way to Jerusalem. It was on this occasion that the two fiery sons of Zebedee, James and John (Jesus called them 'Sons of Thunder', thunder-boys), asked Jesus to allow them to call down 'fire from heaven to burn them up', to avenge this insult to their Master. Jesus 'turned and rebuked them': 'You do not know of what spirit you are' (cf. Lk 9:54-5).

The parallels with our situation in this land are surely close and do not need to be spelled out. But we should all reflect deeply on these parallels. We should especially reflect on the radical transformation wrought by Jesus in terms of attitudes and relations between Jews and Samaritans. One sign of this is the change, the conversion, of John from young firebrand to beloved disciple and disciple of love; the John who spoke tirelessly of Jesus' new commandment of love, the practice of which was to be the distinctive mark of the disciples of Jesus; the John who, in his old age, wore himself and his people out preaching constantly about love. The elder John's one theme of preaching was: 'Little children, love one another.' When people grumbled about this monotonous repetition, he would reply: 'But that is the whole of the Master's teaching, nothing else is needed.'

Jew and Gentile

In Ephesians 2:12 the Gentiles are described as 'having no hope and without God in the world'. In this context it is interesting to consider the attitude of Cahal Daly to the world of unbelief. He encouraged engagement with secularist thinking, reminding his university students that 'the unexamined life is not worth living'. He promoted the study of modern European thought as fervently as the study of Greek philosophy and medieval scholarship. He found in the writings of secular existentialists, like Sartre and Camus, 'remarkable articulations of the religious and spiritual and moral consequences of the social and cultural changes influencing society in western Europe'.

The second great division in the time of Jesus was the even deeper division between Jew and Gentile. There is not time now to reflect at length on this. It is enough to recall how St Paul, himself a Jew of impeccable ancestry and formation, found a new identity in Christ, where Jewishness is not denied or abolished, but is transformed into a 'new creation' in Christ (cf. 2 Cor 5:17). In Christ henceforth there is 'neither Jew nor Gentile'; both are reconciled and become one new thing in Christ (cf. Gal 3:28).

The cost of this reconciliation, this new creation, is crucifixion. Jesus broke down the dividing walls between Jew and Gentile by the hammer blows that pierced His hands; He nailed the divisions to His Cross; He took the stripes of the hatreds on His own bare and bleeding back; He destroyed the hostility in His body, taking its spear-point directly on His own heart (cf. Eph 2:14; Col 2:14).

Love is costing. We know what it cost Jesus; as one of the saints remarked: 'My love is crucified.'

Reconciliation

From 1974 Cahal Daly was a member of the Pontifical Council for Promoting Christian Unity and in 1979 he wrote an open letter to Protestants in which he appealed to them 'to believe that no community in Western Europe is likely to be as sympathetic and supportive towards your Protestant religious beliefs and principles as are Irish Catholics'. He continued, 'Irish Protestants and Irish Catholics can and must help one another to stay faithful to Christ in a world where more and more people walk away from Him.'

In an obituary on 1 January 2010 The Times *suggested that no Catholic bishop did more than Cardinal Daly to bring different denominations together in Northern Ireland. Rev. Dr John Dunlop, a former moderator of the Presbyterian Church in Ireland, described Cahal as 'a clear Christian leader, a warm-hearted friend and a fair-minded, courageous and persuasive advocate for change, for whose work and witness all the people of Ireland, including Presbyterians, have cause to thank God'.*

Reconciliation is always a religious imperative. Catholics have special responsibilities in respect of ecumenical outreach at this time. Individually and collectively each of us and each of our communities must become active agents of reconciliation, especially with our Protestant neighbours. For a variety of historical and theological reasons, the Roman Catholic Church seems to inspire fear and suspicion in the minds of some Protestants. Some of this is undoubtedly the result of sectarianism, which is still an active and evil force in our society, even though all the Churches are officially committed to eliminating it. Some of this sectarianism is still, sadly, being disseminated from some platforms and even from a few pulpits. Some of it is, we Catholics are convinced, due to misunderstanding by others of what we Catholics believe. We must make serious efforts to understand our own faith better, so as to be able to give convincing reasons for the hope that is in us. Above all, we must try much harder to live our own faith better, so that our lives may themselves serve to allay the fears and dispel the suspicions of others.

In the name of the whole Catholic Church, there have been calls by Popes for repentance on the part of Catholics, for Catholic sins against the ecumenical spirit. The word 'repent' resounds across the whole of the Bible and particularly in the New Testament. It is a call to radical costing change – a change of heart, a change of our ways of thinking, our ways of relating to others, our ways of living. St Paul called it a 'spiritual revolution' (Eph 4:23-4). The change was to inaugurate a whole new way of relating to persons and to communities felt to be different.

Reconciliation between our communities must have forgiveness at its heart. Our Catholic community has many wrongs to ask forgiveness for, from God and from the Protestant and unionist community. We also have suffered many wrongs for which we must forgive the Protestant and unionist communities. The Protestant community has to reflect on the wrongs which members of that community have inflicted on Catholics and has to ask forgiveness from God and the Catholic and nationalist community.

Forgiveness is not easy. It is easy to forgive verbally, but harder to forgive unconditionally and from the heart. It is easy to speak words of forgiveness in the name of others, for hurts and wrongs we have not personally endured. We cannot genuinely ask forgiveness from others until we have felt the pain and listened to the hurt and tried to heal the wounds which the others have endured. But forgiveness is at the heart of our Christian faith. Forgiveness is central in the teaching and example of Jesus Christ, our Lord. Indeed, our faith teaches that only God can forgive sins. Jesus tells us to love others and specifically our enemies as He loves us. Only Jesus Christ, living in us, can make it possible for us to love those who have wronged us and to forgive those who have murdered or maimed our dear ones. Without forgiveness, there can be no peace and no peace process, and the forgiveness must come from within both of our communities. There are many unhealed wounds in both communities. We must try to become healers; and the most efficacious healer is the wounded healer.

Ecumenism is deeply biblical. It has its foundations in Holy Scripture and draws its truest inspiration from God's revealed Word. The Bible, which has so often seemed to divide us, must instead become our common source of commitment for growing together towards oneness in Christ in whom God has 'in our own time, the last days, spoken to us' (Heb 1:1-2).

Love as a Political Imperative

To let Christ into our political situation is to let love into our situation. To be directed by His Spirit is to seek and to strive after peace. Love must inform our politics as well as our personal behaviour if we are to be truly Christian. Love is the first political imperative for the Christian.

Sometimes we are ready to say: 'I'll forgive them if they first admit their crimes and apologise.' But it is often our own prior willingness to forgive which causes others to realise that they were wrong and did wrong. If each party insists that the other must move first, then there will be no movement at all, all change is blocked, all parties are paralysed. God always forgives us first, as He loves us first; and it is His forgiveness and His love which call us to see our need to be forgiven and our need to receive and to accept God's forgiveness. We must as Christians be prepared to make the first move, to take the first step, as well as to walk the extra mile, always ready to take risks, always prepared for rebuff and refusal. The Christian cannot demand that 'the others' first change before loving them; 'the others' can be changed only by our first loving them as they are. The Christian cannot lay down conditions for loving.

The norm of Christian love is described by St Paul as:

> always patient and kind … never rude or selfish; it does not take offence and is not resentful …; it is always ready to excuse, to trust, to hope and to endure whatever comes. (1 Cor 13:4-7)

With Jesus, our Lord and Master, the Christian must every day 'resolutely take the road to Jerusalem' (cf. Lk 9:51). For the Christian, as for Jesus, it will inevitably be a Via Dolorosa; but it is also the way of salvation for ourselves and the Churches, the way to glory, for each of us and for our Churches, in Christ Jesus with the Father. Let our prayer be:

> Glory be to Him whose power, working in us, can do infinitely more than we can ask or imagine; glory be to Him, from generation to generation in the Church and in Christ Jesus for ever and ever. Amen. (Eph 3: 20-1)

Love of Creation

Cahal Daly grew up in rural Co. Antrim at a time when waste of any kind was abhorred. He described the culture of his childhood and boyhood as a 'culture of the reusable or recyclable [in contrast to] the culture of the disposable'. He was steeped in an awareness of the teaching of successive popes on the environment – from Pope St Paul VI's description in 1971 of ecological concern as a 'tragic consequence' of lack of control of human conduct to Pope St John Paul II's call in 1979 for a global ecological conversion. His World Day of Peace homily on 1 January 1990 was entitled 'Caring for the Earth: A Work of Peace', in which he described the earth as our 'common and only, fragile and beautiful home'. One of the Cardinal's last books was The Minding of Planet Earth, *published by Veritas in 2004, in which he reminded us that we are stewards, not masters, of the universe. It could be concluded that the Cardinal was ahead of his time when one reflects that this publication preceded by eleven years the influential encyclical* Laudato Si' *issued on 24 May 2015 by Pope Francis to promote care for our common home.*

It is sometimes wrongly suggested that the Genesis story of creation bears some responsibility for the ravaging of the planet and the reckless exploitation of its resources. That is to forget that the human mandate from God in Genesis is a stewardship, to be exercised under the Law of God. Man and woman are shepherds of creation, gardeners who are set by God in the garden of creation 'to cultivate and take care of it' (Gn 2:15). God made us stewards, and not plunderers, of the earth. We can truly say that ecology as a moral and religious responsibility is firmly established from the very first book of the Bible.

Pope John Paul II spoke in 1990 about the growing awareness of the 'lack of due respect for nature, of the plundering of natural resources', insisting that the ecological crisis has moral implications. The term 'ecology' derives from the Greek word for 'home' reminding us that planet earth is our home which we share with the rest of the human family. We are morally responsible for the effect our behaviour has on the other members of the human family who share with us the same planetary home. This home has resources adequate to meet the basic needs of all, but the resources are not unlimited and are not indestructible. If we irresponsibly waste or destroy or pollute a common resource of humanity – such as water, air, soil, and the conditions which make these elements life-bearing – then we inflict harm and injustice upon other human beings now living and upon future generations as well; in other words, we commit sin.

We have to learn once more that there are material limits to earth's resources and moral limits to our use of them, imposed by respect for the rights of others and by reverence for God, the Creator. What is needed is that those involved in science and technology and the leaders of industry should take very seriously their responsibility for the human habitat, for the welfare of the earth and its atmosphere, for the whole environment. Science, technology and industry, developed indiscriminately and divorced from ethical norms and from a sense of moral responsibility, can endanger the whole future of the planet.

Such dangers include the hole in the ozone layer of the earth's atmosphere, which may already hold mortal danger for the health and even survival of future generations. The ozone layer is affected by the use of certain fertilisers and of propellants used in aerosol cans and refrigerants.

Other examples abound including the indiscriminate use of hormones in animals intended for human consumption and of chemicals in food production and additives in food processing, the release of pollutants into waterways and untreated sewage or oil spillage and industrial waste into our seas. Unrestricted burning of bituminous coal and of fossil fuels can no longer be justified. Grave harm to the environment is also caused by uncontrolled deforestation and especially the reckless destruction of the rain forests, soil erosion and salination of the soil through excessive irrigation.

Crimes against the environment are often expressions of greed, the desire for greater and quicker profit. They are crimes committed by richer and more powerful nations, corporations and individuals against the poor. How can we tolerate without protest a situation where the terms of trade of our vaunted global market economy are stacked against the poorer nations, whose import and export prices are both fixed by the wealthier nations, and fixed to the advantage of the wealthier nations? In a globalised economy, where corporations relocate to wherever they can find workers willing to work for the lowest wages, investors with a conscience will – or should – be careful where they invest and shoppers where and what they purchase.

The Bible has many prayers – for example, the Psalms and the Canticle of Creation in Daniel (Dn 3:51-90) – inspired by wonder at the majesty and beauty of creation and filled with praise and thanksgiving offered to God for and on behalf of creation. In his poem 'Pied Beauty', Gerard Manley Hopkins reflects biblical creation prayers when he gives 'glory to God for dappled things' in their endless variety, which 'He fathers forth whose beauty is past change' and when he sings of the 'dearest freshness deep down things' which comes from the creative work of the Holy Spirit who 'broods over the bent world with warm breast and with ah! bright wings'.

The wonderful *Canticle of Brother Sun* of St Francis of Assisi is an outstanding example of creation prayer and should be familiar to all who are concerned about ecology:

> Most high, all powerful, all good Lord!
> All praise is Yours, all glory, all honour and blessing. ...
> All praise be Yours, my Lord, through all that You have made,
> And first my Lord Brother Sun,
> Who brings the day and light You give us through him. ...
> All praise be Yours, my Lord, through Sister Earth, my Mother,
> Who feeds us in her sovereignty ...

A Catholic approach to ecology could scarcely be complete without reference to Mary, Mother of God, whom the Church salutes as *Regina Coeli*, Queen of Heaven, Queen of the Universe. We can confidently entrust to her motherly care and to her prayers the task of caring for the earth, our fragile and beautiful home.

The wide embrace of the Christian imperative of love from family life through life in the community, including the public and political square, to the care of creation, to the life of worship of the God who is the source and summit of love, was a constant teaching in the work of Cardinal Daly. He often focused on seeing

God and loving him in each neighbour and in each created good we chance to encounter in the here and now.

Profession of Faith

The following profession of faith, based on that used by the Latin American bishops at their General Conference in Mexico in 1979, was often used by Cahal Daly and was adapted by him for use in Ireland.

God is present and alive in Jesus Christ,
The liberator in the heart of Ireland.
We believe in the power of the gospel.
We believe in the power of the Lord Jesus Christ
that suffuses life and moves us towards conversion
and solidarity.
We believe in hope, which nourishes and fortifies
human beings on their way to God our Father.
We believe in the civilisation of love.

CHAPTER 4

Catholic Education

Cahal Daly had a passionate interest in Catholic education nurtured in the home and incarnated in religious schools, inspired by a theocentric approach to the whole curriculum. One of his first Lenten pastoral letters as bishop of Ardagh and Clonmacnois, which was written in marvellously simple blank verse, was on the role of parents in handing on the faith. He recognised the fundamental rights of parents in education and encouraged the choice of a school that aimed to bring about a synthesis of faith and life. The creation of that synthesis was to be achieved through the ethos of the school, in the whole curriculum and not just in the religious education classes. The work of the religious education class was promoted by the Cardinal particularly in his role as president of the Irish Episcopal Commission on Catechetics. He led the development of new religious education programmes for both primary and post-primary schools for the whole of Ireland. Those programmes pioneered a radically new experiential approach that sought to enable children and young people to see every aspect of their lives as a gift from a loving and forgiving God calling them into a relationship of love and prayer with him through Jesus Christ. The material and books from those programmes were displayed along with those from other countries at the synod of bishops in Rome in 1977 on the theme of 'Catechetics in Our Time' and were regarded as superior to those from other countries in terms of content, presentation and methodology.

The Aim of Catholic Education

The aim of Catholic education is to make Christ so real, so living, so personal, for children and young people, that He will be their Lord and King, not just in words but in everyday reality, so that, habitually and almost instinctively, they will speak with Christ in prayer, consult Him in their choices and decisions, turn to Him in their needs and be true to Him as their closest friend in all their difficulties.

Most of the modern popes have issued major encyclicals on Catholic education, and the Second Vatican Council devoted a special declaration to this theme. The Council's teaching has been reinforced by a series of documents issued by the Holy See dealing with topics such as *the Catholic school, the calling of the Catholic teacher* and *the role of the Church in higher education.*

The Vatican Council said:

> The Church is under an obligation to provide for its children an education by virtue of which their whole lives may be inspired by the spirit of Christ. By doing so, the Church will at the same time be offering a service to all peoples by promoting the full development of the human person, thereby enriching human society and contributing to the development of a world more worthy of humanity.

This is an exalted ideal. It might be thought too idealistic, too remote from the realities of an educator's day-to-day pressures and frustrations. There can in practice be great gaps between ideal and reality in Catholic education and we must face up to these shortcomings honestly and realistically. All of us who are in any way responsible for Catholic education – teachers, bishops, priests – must do everything in our power to make our schools more and more truly Christian and Catholic, to go on trying to improve the quality of both religious and secular education in our schools and to work more and more closely with parents in the great task of Catholic education which we share.

The Home as the First School

The home is, of course, the first school, the first religion class. The Vatican Council says quite clearly that the parents are the child's first religion teachers. There are many ways in which this teaching can take place in the Catholic home. For example, just as we display photographs and souvenirs of people who are dear and important to us, there can be visible reminders in our home of God as our Father and Mary as Mother over all of us. Family prayer said together by parents and children should be a regular feature of life. Parents' prayer with and for children should begin even before their birth. There used to be a common saying that an expectant mother has to 'eat for two'. She certainly has to 'pray for two'. We should rather say she has to pray for three, because it is the father and the mother who are expecting the baby, which is 'our baby' not just 'my baby'.

A special feature of Catholic schools, especially at primary level, is their very close link with the parish and the home.

When the child does begin to go to school, the parents and the home must support the work of the school, and particularly the work of religious education in which they should take a close interest. We have been putting great efforts into involving parents in the preparation of children for the sacraments. Meetings of parents before their baby's baptism, before their child's first confession or communion, and before confirmation, are being held successfully in every parish. Parents are taking part in large numbers and I compliment and thank them for this. We ask God to bless all parents in their calling to hand on the faith to their children and young people.

Parents must not leave this task to the school and to the teachers; teachers cannot do this without the support of the home. If the children do not find religion in the lives of their parents and their home, they will not learn religion at school either. If the example of the parents and the experience which the children have at home contradict what is taught in school, the work of the teachers is gravely undermined. If children do not learn about God and prayer at home, it will be a very difficult task for any priest or teacher or school to teach them later to know and love God and to pray.

Even the best of Catholic schools, even the most dedicated teachers, even the most excellent religion programmes, will not make good Christians and good Catholics of our children and young people unless they are supported by the faith of the parents, the home and the parish. The Vatican Council addressed parents directly reminding them of 'their duty to entrust their children to Catholic schools … to support such schools to the extent of their ability and to work along with them for the welfare of the children'.

We thank God for the great blessings brought to our whole community by our Catholic schools. Not only do they provide our children with a secular education second to none – and all parents naturally wish their children to have the best possible education for their children, since this is the best foundation for their careers and prospects of employment. But, what is much more important, our Catholic schools provide our children with the best conditions for learning and living the faith, which is our greatest gift from God. Parents have no greater gift to hand on to their children than the gift of faith.

It is right for parents to be concerned about good examination grades and academic successes and post-school career opportunities. But parents must never seek these at the expense of their children's formation in the faith. It would be sad if Catholic parents were to show interest only in a school's standards in secular subjects and accomplishments, and not equally in its work in religious education. Our schools are the greatest help parents could have for handing on the faith.

The Value and Importance of Catholic Schools

The Declaration on Christian Education of the Vatican Council says:

> Among all the agencies of education the school has a special importance. By virtue of its very purpose, while the school cultivates the intellect with unremitting attention, it develops the capacity for sound judgement and introduces the pupils to the cultural heritage bequeathed to them by former generations. It fosters a sense of values and prepares pupils for professional life. ... It encourages mutual understanding.

The value and importance which the Catholic Church attaches to the Catholic school have been strongly and repeatedly emphasised by the teaching authority of the Church. The emphasis on Catholic schools for Catholic children is not something peculiar to Ireland. It is the teaching of the Catholic Church worldwide and is the practice of the Church right across the world. All through history, the Catholic educational system has been the greatest strength of the faith in a country. Governments and regimes which want to suppress the Catholic religion always begin by suppressing Catholic schools. The decline of Catholic education in any country is always followed by the decline of faith and religious practice in that country. Where there are no Catholic schools, secularism spreads very rapidly.

The document on the Catholic school, issued by the Congregation for Catholic Education, speaks of the school as being oriented towards a:

> Christian concept of life centred on Jesus Christ. Christ is the foundation of the whole educational enterprise in a Catholic school. Christ's revelation gives new meaning to life and helps men and women to direct their thought, action and will according to the Gospel. … The task of the Catholic school is fundamentally to bring about a synthesis of culture and faith and a synthesis of faith and life: the first is reached by seeking to integrate all the different aspects of human knowledge through the subjects taught; the second through the development of the virtues characteristic of the Christian.

In a Catholic school, religion is not just one slot in the curriculum. The whole atmosphere of the school is religious. The visits of priests to the school give the children the chance of getting to know their priests from their earliest years, and this has an influence in their future lives. Masses in the school, school and class prayers, religious pictures on the walls, the statue of Our Lady, the 'May altar', the Advent wreath and the Lenten pictures of the Passion or the Stations of the Cross, the children's religion projects in the classroom, school and class visits to the church, all these are ways of teaching the faith which are just as important as the formal religion class.

Academic success is important, but we must not make it the sole or even the main criterion in our evaluation of teachers or our classification of schools. A still more important service is given to the community by the dedication which a school staff shows towards its less academically gifted students. This has a very salutary influence in improving the morale and the confidence of children and their parents and their families, especially in deprived urban neighbourhoods. This is a profoundly Christian witness. In a Christian and Catholic school system it is not the academically gifted but rather the educationally and socially deprived pupils who should be the objects of greatest care and concern. No praise is too high for the work of our teachers in many demoralised inner-city or new-estate parishes. They deserve the gratitude of the whole community and the support of the parish and the home in their work.

The contribution made by the Catholic school to the work of the Church and to the welfare of society is inestimable and is deserving of admiration and gratitude from the whole Catholic community. Indeed, this contribution deserves greater public recognition than it sometimes seems to receive.

The Catholic School and Reconciliation in Society

From the beginning of his time as bishop of Down and Connor, Cahal Daly was most appreciative of the work of Catholic schools as beacons of hope and oases of calm in the midst of the civil disturbances. He saw as unfair suggestions that Catholic schools caused division in Northern Ireland and often advocated on behalf of the role of Catholic schools in promoting mutual understanding.

Catholic schools are sometimes called 'divisive'. Public discussion and media comment sometimes seems to suggest that in Northern Ireland Catholic schools are in their effect, if not by their very existence, factors for continuing division in the community. It seems almost to be implied that those who support Catholic education are, by that very fact, obstacles to reconciliation between our communities. Advocates of integrated education sometimes speak as if they, almost alone in the educational field, are working effectively for reconciliation in society. I wish that people could come to realise how offensive and hurtful any such suggestions can be to Catholic teachers and how unfair to Catholic schools.

Catholic schools have been, through the bitter years of conflict in Northern Ireland, strong factors for stability and normality, at times when conditions in society brought serious risk of instability and in areas where powerful forces were actively working for destabilisation. Particularly in the most deprived areas and often in very stressful circumstances, Catholic teachers succeeded in creating oases of peace in the midst of community violence; they have instilled love and forgiveness where others in the community were fomenting hate; they maintained classroom discipline where all around were the elements of indiscipline and disorder, disruption and lawlessness. The entire community is indebted to these teachers, who maintained high scholastic standards, and at the same time instilled attitudes of love and peace in situations of rampant violence and social unrest.

Catholic teachers have been and are devoting their best energies to the inculcation of attitudes of Christian love and forgiveness, peace and non-violence and reconciliation. These values serve indeed to define the ethos of the Catholic school. Our schools are doing all they can to foster a spirit of reconciliation and good neighbourliness by seeking contact with schools in the controlled and Protestant voluntary sectors and enabling children and young people of both communities to get to know and to respect each other. Parents can thus be assured that their children have the advantage of a solid foundation in their own faith and the opportunity of learning tolerance and understanding of the faith of others. It is our firm view that Catholic schools would be failing in their mission if they were not also committed to the principles of respect for different religious traditions and actively involved in ecumenical outreach and in cross-community contact between teachers and pupils. Catholic teachers will be found in the forefront of all activities designed to multiply cross-community contacts and shared projects at school level. Truth and justice demand that this be recognised.

The gradual progress towards equity in the provision of educational facilities, acceptable to Catholics and to Protestants respectively, has been an important factor in the struggle for equality of treatment and parity of esteem between the two traditions in Ireland, particularly in Northern Ireland, and this itself has made a significant contribution to reconciliation.

A Pioneering Catechetical Programme

Cahal Daly had a passion for teaching from his first appointment to the Department of Classics in St Malachy's College, Belfast, in September 1944 until he left his post as reader in scholastic philosophy at Queen's University, Belfast, when appointed bishop of Ardagh and Clonmacnois in 1967. He felt that his early teaching was 'rather conventional and pedantic, depending too much on traditional textbooks and too little enriched by personal exploration' and succeeded in modernising his approach to the great appreciation of his third-level students in Belfast. As president of the Episcopal Commission on Catechetics, he was delighted to have the opportunity to lead a similar transition in the teaching of religion in Ireland. The change was in essence from a teacher-centred dependence on rote learning to a learner-centred and experience-based journey towards a knowing, loving and prayerful relationship with God in Jesus Christ. It was a radical change that was not always understood and was sometimes criticised as not being sufficiently theologically focused. It was, however, widely recognised both in Ireland and internationally as an exciting and pioneering project.

The most ambitious catechetical renewal programme ever attempted in Ireland was decided on by the Irish Bishops in the 1970s. The programme envisaged the provision of a complete set of catechetical resource materials extending from infant school to adult religious education groups. It can modestly be claimed that few countries have attempted so comprehensive a catechetical project.

The project was designed to meet the long-felt need and desire for a new approach offering teachers a real choice and the possibility of adjusting their teaching materials and methods to the varying interests of their pupils.

The new approach favoured beginning with the life-experience of the pupils and going on to show how religion relates to this experience and how the experience itself points to God and to our relationship with God. This was not simply an attempt to hold the pupil's interest; the method itself taught something vitally important about Christianity: that Christianity is for living and that all living has to be made Christian. Christianity is not adequately presented if Christian doctrine is ever isolated from Christian living. A great merit of the new programme was that at every point it showed the implications of each doctrinal theme for the way we should behave, as individuals and as a society. If religion cannot be seen by young people to fit, to explain, to inspire and to help here and now, it will tend always to remain divorced from life.

The whole justification of life-centred catechetics, the whole thrust of the new Irish Catechetical Programme might be found in the words of St Paul: 'To me to live is Christ.'

We cannot teach the God who is love and the Christ who is God's love, given for human beings, in an atmosphere of anger, ill-temper or impatience on the part of the teacher, or of fear, resentment or internal bickering on the part of the pupils. That is why the programme placed such emphasis on the life of the class group and the atmosphere of the class situation. The class has to be the Gospel at work now; it ought to be the Spirit of Christ forming a Christian community in this particular group of believers now.

The word enthusiasm in its earliest roots implies being filled with the excitement and joy of God. Without this enthusiasm on the part of teachers and pupils there can be no credible transmission of the Good News about Jesus Christ, the Son of God, or about the Christian Way, that new way of thinking, living, praying and celebrating which Jesus Christ brought into our tired world.

The Service of Teachers to Society

I wish to pay tribute as Bishop to the Catholic teachers as a body, past and present, retired and active, for their contribution. We can never fully assess or express what we owe to them. In the last analysis, it is teachers who determine the quality of education, much more than governments or administrators, planners or sociologists, even buildings or equipment. It is the faith conviction and the Christian lives of teachers that determine whether and to what extent a school is Catholic. Indeed, no one is more conscious of the difficulties in realising the ideal than Catholic teachers are, although the difficulties are, by and large, not of their making and not under their control or in their power to remedy.

It is unfortunate that the impression is sometimes given that Government has been more conscious of the defects in the existing educational system than of its merits and has been more prone to blame teachers for those defects than to give them credit for its achievements. I am sure that this is by no means intended and that the impression is erroneous. It would help, however, if public tribute were more often paid to the teaching profession and if the huge difficulties which confront teachers in modern society were more readily recognised. There are disturbing signs of a crisis of morale in the teaching profession. It is vital that teachers receive not only deserved affirmation of their work and due recognition of their difficulties, but also and especially that they receive additional resources commensurate with the demands of their work and are awarded scales of remuneration corresponding to their important role in society and sufficient to attract into their profession and retain within it women and men of the highest calibre.

Society imposes heavy responsibilities on teachers. It does not always show sufficient appreciation of the service they give. In present-day conditions, the work of teachers has become much more difficult than formerly. Many of our pupils see no prospect of jobs at the end of their school days. The experience of many Catholic children is that, however hard they work at school, however successful their examination results, they simply will not be given fair or equal opportunities in the job market. This experience inevitably creates a crippling sense of apathy and hopelessness among pupils. It saps motivation for study. It is doing much to undermine the confidence of young people in their future. It is engendering a feeling among them that society does not care for them and has no place for them. Young people are the greatest resource of any society. For a society which purports to be a caring society, we are showing too little care and concern for young people and are offering them little hope for the future.

This has serious repercussions for the work of teachers. It is more difficult than ever for them to inculcate motivation and inspire enthusiasm among their pupils. Teachers can be forgiven for feeling that they are being left to cope in the classroom with problems created by the wider society, and that, at the same time, that society is depriving them of resources and conditions needed to help and to cope with these problems. Cutbacks in education could not be coming at a more inopportune time. They are tantamount to a policy of disinvestment in our future. Another source of grave apprehension and even demoralisation among teachers in many places, particularly in urban areas and in the secondary sector, is the factor of falling enrolments, with the redundancies and threat of redundancies which this brings in its train. Security of employment served in the past as non-pecuniary compensation for salaries which have always been modest in comparison with those of people of corresponding qualifications or in correspondingly important areas of service to society. Society does not reward teachers adequately for the work they do. In fact, teachers' salaries have, for many years past, been falling steadily in relation to the incomes of other sectors of employment with which they once enjoyed parity. Teachers cannot but conclude that society puts less and less value on their work, at the same time as their work becomes more difficult and more demanding. A society which cares for its children must also show greater care for the teachers to whom we entrust our children.

It is surely a measure of the frustration of teachers that they feel driven to the sad expedient of school strikes, as a means of vindicating their claims. It is sincerely to be hoped that government and teachers' unions will quickly arrive at settlement terms which will prevent strikes, put new heart into teachers, and assure them of society's appreciation of their work for our children, and will spare our children and young people the added handicap of interrupted classes.

It remains true, however, that people are drawn to the teaching profession, not by considerations of financial gain but primarily out of a sense of vocation. Teaching is a noble Christian vocation. The teacher shares with Our Lord himself the noble title of 'Teacher', 'Master'. In a very real sense, the work of the teacher is a sharing in the work of Christ himself; it is a vital part of the preparation for 'the new heavens and the new earth' which He came to inaugurate. In a special way teachers can see Christ as the prototype of their profession and can take Him as their role model in their task. Jesus put His arms around the little children who were brought to Him by their parents, laid His hands on them and gave them His blessing. Surely that blessing of the Lord goes also to the teachers who bring little ones to Jesus, introduce them to Him and teach them to love Him.

I pray today that many of our best young Catholic men and women will find in the teaching vocation their call to Christian apostolate and will find in it the path to holiness to which, by baptism, all of us are called.

The teacher is often said to stand *in loco parentis*. I suggest that, above all, the teacher stands *in loco Christi*, stands before his or her pupils in the place of Christ, represents Christ to his or her class. The teacher speaks Christ to the pupils, is Christ for them. The teacher must be able to say to his or her pupils, as St Paul said: 'Keep doing all the things that you learnt from me and have been taught by me and have heard or seen that I do. Then the God of peace will be with you' (Phil 4:9).

Catholic teachers, and specifically lay Catholic teachers, have been and are one of the greatest resources and strengths of the Catholic Church in Ireland. The Church's debt to them is immense; our gratitude to them is profound.

Mary, the mother of Jesus, formed her Son in human knowledge of the Scriptures and of the history of God's plan for His people and in adoration of the Father. 'And Jesus grew in wisdom and stature and in favour with God and all the people' (Lk 2:52). Mary has been described as 'a living catechism' and 'the mother and model of catechists'. May her prayers give us confidence that Our Lord, who did great things for her, will do great things for all involved in the work of Catholic education.

On 2 June 1967 Cahal Daly announced at a press conference in Belfast his appointment as bishop of Ardagh and Clonmacnois. While leaving with sadness the academic work that he loved and where he had been happy as a student and teacher, he looked forward to finding affirmation in his own faith and wisdom of the kind 'not found in libraries or in academic common rooms'. As bishop and cardinal, he often reflected on the importance of Catholic education, begun in the home and continued in the school and in the parish. He promoted the involvement of parents in the parish-based pre-sacramental catechesis of their children. He ushered in a radically new approach to the teaching of religion in the Catholic school. He saw teachers as deriving their title from Christ and encouraged them in their work of helping the young to walk in the light of love so that through them the light of Christ might shine out in the world and overcome the divisions in society.

CHAPTER 5

The Cry of the Poor: The Imperative of Social Justice

Cahal Daly was one of a number of priests who were ordained in Maynooth College Chapel on 22 June 1941. They decided to found Christus Rex, a society of priests dedicated to an understanding of the social teaching of the Catholic Church and to the encouragement of all priests to work for social justice. As chair of Christus Rex for more than twenty years, Cahal promoted the latter aims throughout the whole of Ireland and they became an important part of his episcopal ministry.

Is Religion World-Evading?

Christianity is often accused of having despised and neglected this world because of its preoccupation with 'the next world'. Christians are alleged to be solely absorbed with eternity, not with time, concerned with God and not with humanity. Two of the great sources of modern humanist thought, Karl Marx and Friedrich Nietzsche, agree in making this kind of charge. Marx called religion 'the opium of the people', the pathetic but resigned and impotent 'sigh of the oppressed creature'.

Authentic Christian belief in eternity, of its very nature, could not be an opiate; eternal truths are more likely to call for alarm clocks than for pillows. If Christians ever neglected social involvement, it was not because they loved God too much or because they were too preoccupied with death, judgement and a mortal life. St Peter's First Epistle says: 'The end of all things is at hand.' The writer does not say 'therefore keep your head down, your eyes closed, your arms folded, prepare your soul and wait for the end to come'. What he does say is: 'The end of all things is at hand … therefore use your gifts in the service of God and put yourselves at the service of others.' The acceptance of Christ's salvation in the New Testament always leads to a question and a decision for action: 'What must we do …?' (cf. Acts 2:37).

Among the many issues urgently needing to be faced by the Churches at the present time, I wish to single out two – poverty and unemployment – which call for a response to the latter question.

It might be said that it is little I know about the complexities of economics and politics. A phrase is sometimes used of Church people enunciating moral principles: 'Get real'; 'Join the real world'. Economics and politics, we are told, have their own exigencies, market forces have their own realities; and these are the real world. On the contrary, I suggest that moral principles are the real world; and the people we most admire are those who put moral principle before profit and conscience above career. Economics and politics can be and must be redeemed from their own self-destructive excesses and abuses by men and women of steadfast moral principle.

The Last Judgement, described in the Gospel of St Matthew, will certainly have appalling surprises and shocks for us all. In a modern and developed society, all groups are more closely interdependent than ever before. Every transaction on the stock exchange, every takeover bid, every wealth-accumulating deal, every income or wage increase, every personnel-management failure and every industrial strike inflicts consequences on the other groups in society and especially on the weaker groups. In such a society, there will be less excuse than ever for saying: 'But, Lord, when did we see you hungry or thirsty or naked?'

The new commandment, distinctive of Christ's followers, 'Love one another' has a direct relevance for every decision that is taken by industrialist, manager, employer, worker, farmer, trade-union official in [any economic] crisis. Each decision must be taken in clear awareness of the consequence for others of that decision. It is un-Christian to plan the closing of a factory, the lay-off of workers, the pressing of a wage-claim or the launching of a strike on the basis only of the advantages to my factory or firm or profits or assets, or to my income or pay-packet or differentials or my group of workers, and without equal concern for the effects on employment prospects for others, the cost of living for others, the consequences for our international competitiveness, our international image; for investment, for tourism; the implications for national recovery. [Any economic] crisis is a time for testing whether our Christian profession of love for one another is only airy-fairy talk or is going to affect the way we actually live.

It was St John of the Cross who said that in the evening of life we shall all be judged upon love. But Christian love is not a matter of sentiment or feeling or mere motive and intention; it must strive to be personally effective and socially efficacious. Christ is the just one (cf. Acts 7:52) come amongst us to proclaim God's Kingdom of justice, love and peace. The will of God on earth demands social structuring as well as personal striving. There must be systematic and political involvement from Christians.

The Work of Justice

In 1977 the Irish Catholic Bishops' Conference published a pastoral letter, The Work of Justice. *This section is an extract from that letter. Bishop Joseph Duffy has said that Cahal Daly was the main draftsman of such episcopal statements.*

The Catholic Bishops in Ireland know the social conditions in the communities from which most of the violence emanated. We also know, from our contacts with religious leaders and clergy and people from other denominations, the conditions which bred violence from within certain Protestant communities. There are many features common to both Protestant and Catholic communities where there has been active or tacit support for paramilitaries. Notable among these are poverty, unemployment, social alienation and exclusion, educational deprivation, political powerlessness, and, accompanying these, a cluster of social, familial and community problems. A further feature of such areas is a relatively high rate of imprisonment among members of these communities, and especially among young members, both for paramilitary offences and for ordinary criminal offences. Our experience points to the close correlation between poverty, unemployment, socio-economic deprivation and political powerlessness, on the one hand, and politically motivated violence, on the other, in sectors of both the Catholic and the Protestant communities. A map of Belfast's areas of need will be seen to correlate very closely with a map of the density of incidents of paramilitary violence, as well as other forms of urban violence. Paramilitary violence is in part an expression – albeit an immoral and irrational and inexcusable expression – of anger and protest against social conditions which are degrading to the human person. Violence we must categorically condemn, without exception or qualification or excusation of any kind. But it is not enough to condemn violence unless we also condemn and try to remedy the social inequalities and the social and political injustices which breed violence.

Poverty

Poverty is one important factor in a whole cluster of interrelated social problems, including drugs and alcohol abuse, violent crime, violence against women and children, marital break-up and family instability, teenage pregnancy. Poverty creates what have been called wastelands of human dignity, which are found particularly in areas of urban blight but also in areas of rural decay. There are many boats in this country which have not been lifted up by any rising economic tide; there are many areas which have not shared in any economic boom. Poverty in both communities takes similar forms, has similar causes and produces similar effects. Deprivation – moral, psychological, educational, environmental and familial – has increased tragically in recent years, due to violence, due to the run-down and wreckage of inner-city areas, more recently due to economic cut-backs. There is now a great mass of human misery in many areas, Protestant as well as Catholic. A plan to reduce and ultimately eliminate poverty in both areas should and could unite people from both communities in a movement of joint Christian and human commitment to social justice.

One of the unfortunate developments in modern society, particularly in the larger cities, is that of the increasing physical and spatial segregation of the richer from the poorer communities. It is sad that the living conditions of the poor are almost totally unknown to those living in more prosperous areas. It seems to be chiefly when certain areas are associated with violence or vandalism, street rioting or crime, that the existence of these areas and the living conditions within them come to public attention. In such circumstances, public demand is often limited to a call that violence and vandalism be curbed, for example by measures such as increased police presence, more severe penalties for crime, 'short, sharp, shock' treatment of young offenders, etc. When or if such measures are effective to the extent that offences against persons and property diminish, many people, sometimes even the police, seem to be happy that a problem has been solved. But it is at best only symptoms that have been brought under control. The underlying causes of anti-social behaviour have not been even touched. The public conscience should be as deeply concerned about the conditions in which people in poorer or run-down areas live, the conditions in which their children grow up, as they are about their own right to unmolested freedom of movement and protection of property.

The terrible fact is that the selective material progress which our society has made and is making not only widens the income gap between rich and poor, it also tends to increase the geographical and especially the psychological distance between their places of residence. Contact and communication across the socio-economic boundaries are no less necessary than they are across the religious denominations within those boundaries. I believe that precisely this form of contact and communication is specifically important for justice and peace in this land.

On 10 May 1989, almost twelve years after the publication of The Work of Justice, *at a conference sponsored by the Corrymeela Community and the Irish School of Ecumenics entitled 'Facing the Challenge: Roman Catholic and Evangelical Response to Social Issues', Bishop Daly reflected with some pain and disappointment at the relative lack of response to the challenges enunciated in that pastoral.*

I was one of the Catholic Bishops who called in 1977 for 'a national programme to eliminate poverty'. One is humbled, and indeed embarrassed, to re-read that call many years further on. Poverty has not lessened; indeed, it has increased. The gap between the rich and the poor has widened. More people are caught now than then in a 'poverty trap' from which it is impossible for them to escape by their own unaided resources. Yet the reality of poverty is largely ignored by governments and by politicians, while media seem increasingly fascinated by the life-style of the super-rich and by movements in the money and property markets.

Church people, including Bishops, and Church committees, including Inter-Church conferences and committees, are better at formulating fine declarations and resolutions than they are at implementing them. We tend to feel that we have 'had a good meeting', 'faced resolutely up to a problem', when we have only issued a trenchant press release or produced a challenging report.

Politicians often proclaim priority for action in the inner cities but too often such proclamations are nothing more than rhetorical flourish. The rehabilitation of decayed inner-city areas in both parts of Ireland is still awaiting cohesive planning and action from Government and local authorities, and commitment from the private sector. It is when communities crumble and atomise, losing cohesion, self-confidence and self-respect, that symptoms of social sickness, such as vandalism, 'joy-riding', gang violence, school truancy, alcoholism, drug-addiction, tend to manifest themselves.

Community development is the key to the alleviation of many social evils of today. The creation of community where the sense of community does not exist; the preservation and strengthening of existing real communities where they do exist, whether in rural or in urban areas; the avoidance of policies and the resisting of trends which break up existing communities, should be a first concern of all social planning. Planning is for people, for communities, rather than for production targets or progress reports. The Church, which lays such emphasis on community, the Church, which is itself essentially community, has a great responsibility and a splendid opportunity in this regard.

The poor should themselves be involved in plans for the rehabilitation of their own areas and their own lives. Poor persons must not be merely objects of research and planning. They must be not only recipients of subsidies and grants. They must be motivated to be agents of their own amelioration. Their dignity as persons must be respected. Their intelligence and their sense of their own problems and needs must be deployed. Community decay has been a large cause of their condition, community rehabilitation will be a large part of the remedy; and communities are rehabilitated largely by becoming actively involved in their own self-rehabilitation.

The entire community must, however, become conscious of its collective responsibility for the poor in our midst. The poor do not deserve to be poor. Neither do they just happen to be poor. First of all, in many cases, they were programmed for poverty, often long before their birth; programmed by a history of parental misfortune or neglect, parental unemployment or educational deprivation, parental alcoholism, marital separation, illness or physical handicap, child abuse. What is still more disturbing is that the poor are being made poor and are being kept poor by the very same factors which are making other people in the same sector richer.

Unemployment

Unemployment is one of the major social problems in our society and is the greatest single source of poverty for individuals and families. The Churches must challenge their communities in respect of commonly held stereotyped attitudes towards the unemployed and in respect of society's responsibilities towards the unemployed.

Those with jobs are privileged; often they are those whom society has favoured and subsidised, giving them better education and better opportunities. In modern society, it is very largely a myth that people succeed primarily because of their superior entrepreneurial spirit, their self-drive and self-reliance. Such qualities are undeniably an element in business and professional success. They must not lead us to ignore, however, the immense contribution made by the taxpayer, namely by society as a whole, to every business or professional success story. Every industrial enterprise now benefits from massive public subsidy, both in terms of direct grant and in terms of tax relief and tax incentive. Every industrial worker is a beneficiary of State subsidy. Every new industrial job is subsidised. It is paradoxical that industrial grants are regarded as rewards for enterprise, while unemployment benefits are regarded as dole money for the work-shy or for 'welfare-spongers'.

Disparaging remarks about the unemployed as 'being better off idle than working' are almost always untrue, unjustified and injurious. Very few persons choose or prefer to be unemployed. Only in rare cases and for short periods is anyone better off unemployed than working. Unemployment and welfare benefits are no proper substitute for wages. Even an enlightened welfare society is saying to people: 'We will pay you just enough to live on; but we do not really need you. Society can function very well without you. Indeed, you are a burden on society.'

This is demoralising. It is destructive of a person's self-esteem. Unemployment is a cause of tension in marriages and of dissension in families. For the young, a job is a symbol of independence. To have a job is to be an adult, to begin to have one's own earned money and to have some control over one's own life. Not to have a job and never to see hope of a job is to be drawn close to hopelessness. It feeds the spirit of resentment and rebellion.

Our society needs comprehensive and sustained programmes of job creation, particularly in deprived areas. There is still too little evidence of concentrated government and civil service planning, too little evidence of a comprehensive and well-researched economic development plan for deprived areas. While the primary responsibility rests with government, the private sector also has major responsibility for job creation. The public grants, the incentives and the opportunities now being offered to industrialists create for them corresponding and serious moral obligations in the matter of job creation. There must be restraints on income and profits on the part of employers, on the part of entrepreneurs, executives, professional classes, highly skilled and highly paid specialists. There must be effective guarantees and checks to ensure that the incentives and the benefits offered to industrialists are in fact devoted to the purpose which, by public policy, they are intended to serve, namely the creation of new jobs. Excess accruing profits should be ploughed back into new jobs, and the performance of industrialists should be monitored to ensure that the promised new jobs will effectively be created.

Our society must never be allowed to become a haven where the rich have privileged opportunities to become richer and 'the haves' are facilitated to have more. All public economic policy must have a social dimension, a commitment to fairer shares for all.

Both employers and labour should be motivated, not by the 'get rich' mentality, but by the desire to improve social conditions and promote social justice for all. The justification for private ownership of property and of wealth in Christian social teaching is the attainment of fairer shares of the good things of creation for all the sons and daughters of our common Father, 'from whom all good things come'.

West Belfast: Problems and Hopes

The Divis Complex, comprising Divis Tower and 12 eight-storey blocks made up of 850 flats housing 2,400 residents, was built in the 1960s on the lower Falls Road in West Belfast. After only a few years there were calls for the complex, once described in a European Union report as the worst of its kind in Europe, to be demolished. That demolition commenced eventually in the late 1980s and was completed, apart from Divis Tower, in 1994. The complex was located very close to St Peter's Pro-Cathedral.

Having concluded a week-long visitation this March 1985 of St Peter's Parish, I wish to record some of my reactions.

My first reaction is one of unbounded admiration for the people of St Peter's, in the area commonly called the 'Lower Falls'. This area is far too often misrepresented by the media and misjudged by public opinion. It has become associated in some people's minds with violence, rioting and unrest. In particular, the name 'Divis' is made to seem synonymous with lawlessness and crime. It would seem that some who live in other parts of the city would almost hesitate to visit the area.

These attitudes are totally unjustified. They are a slur on the good people who live here. There are unfortunately a few who give the area a bad name, whether by deeds of political violence or by 'ordinary' violence and crime. But they are a minority. The great majority of the people of St Peter's, and of the Divis Complex in particular, are warm-hearted, kind, welcoming, peace-loving people. Their cheerfulness, amidst often depressing surroundings, is remarkable. Their spirit of forgiveness, in spite of bitter experiences, is edifying. Their generosity to the needs of the Church, to the poor and to the Third World, in spite of deep recession, is astonishing. The people of St Peter's and of Divis are among the best people to be found anywhere in Belfast or in Ireland. Society owes them respect and even admiration. Government and public agencies owe them amends for decades of misplanning, broken promises and neglect.

The Divis Complex

The first thing to be said about the Divis Complex is that it should never have been built. No refurbishing will ever make it an acceptable human environment. It stands as a monument to a bad period of urban planning, planning which, however well-intentioned at the time, was disastrously misconceived, and has been demonstrated by experience to have been a source of immense human and community misery. People should not be allowed to go on suffering indefinitely from planning blunders of the past, for which they are in no way responsible.

Following my visit of the Complex, I have to say quite categorically that, in my opinion, there is no acceptable solution to the problems of the Divis Complex other than complete demolition of the flat-blocks, and their replacement by conventional housing.

Let it be said straight away that no reasonable person expects this to be done all at once. It will have to be phased over a period of years. But there must be a firm public commitment that this will be done. Whitehall and Farset Blocks have already been demolished. This was a welcome beginning. It has been announced that St Brendan's and Pound Blocks are to be demolished. This further demolition should be proceeded with rapidly, and the building of new houses in the area thus cleared should be a matter of urgency.

Refurbishing of the remaining flats is undoubtedly necessary. I regret to have to say that the worst of the flats are quite unfit for human habitation and are a disgrace to public housing, and this is by no means the fault of the inhabitants, but is due to structural defects and inadequate or failed maintenance programmes. But refurbishing of the whole complex is an absolute necessity, and this in the shorter rather than in the longer term. The refurbishing must not, however, carry any implication that the Flats are to be left standing for an undefined future. The people of Divis should not be expected to accept refurbishing, if this is taken to imply willingness on their part to live indefinitely in the Flats. Even the refurbished Flats would still be a quite unacceptable environment for decent human community living. The refurbishing programme should be linked with a firm public commitment to the complete replacement of the Flats by normal housing, through a phased programme to be completed by a specified date, within a reasonable time-span.

I am conscious of the financial constraints affecting the Department of the Environment and the Northern Ireland Housing Executive. I am conscious of the fact that they are being asked to 'pick up the tabs' for earlier misplanning for which they were not responsible. But I am still more conscious of the demands of justice and of human rights and the respect due to the dignity of persons and communities. The need for radical action in respect of the Flats has been recognised for years. In 1978 the Planning Team of the Belfast Areas of Need declared:

> The Divis Complex is unique in the city because of its size, because of its high density and high-rise characteristics, and because of the acute social need of many of its occupants.

The following issues were then identified as requiring urgent attention:

> Separation of the deck access blocks, treatment of dampness and condensation, heating, lifts, stairways and walkways, pedestrian-ways, refuse disposal systems, drying areas, open space, car parking, landscape, play areas, general clean up, housing and landscape maintenance, and shopping.

It is now time to admit that the problems are due to basic and incurable structural and planning defects. It is time to admit that the financial cost of maintaining the Flats and the social costs of the human problems created by retaining them far outweigh the cost of demolition and replacement.

Going around Divis, I met numerous families who, from the windows of their flats, were able to point across the street to where they used to live until their houses were burnt and their streets sacked by rampaging loyalist mobs in the early 1970s. By God's grace, they look back without bitterness. Indeed they look back with sorrow for their former good Protestant neighbours who had to look on helplessly but heart-brokenly while all this was being done in the name of Protestantism, but to the shame and disgust of decent Protestants.

I have also to say that the neglect which has permitted the continuing social deterioration of the area has allowed the name of Divis to become a positive obstacle to employment prospects, almost a disqualification for employment, for its residents. Linked with this is the highly disturbing fact that there are indications that an address in West Belfast can be used by the authorities as a pretext for refusing employment to a young person on alleged 'security grounds'.

Excellent New Housing

At this time, I want to record my deep appreciation of the excellent new housing now being provided by the Housing Executive in the Lower Falls area. As houses of this quality replace the older sub-standard houses and are put back where the Flats now stand, the real quality of the people of St Peter's will be seen in its true light, and St Peter's will recover the prestige among Belfast parishes which its people earned down the generations in the past and which they deserve but do not always receive in the present.

Social Problems Compounded by Paramilitary Violence

All our social problems in Divis and in West Belfast are compounded by paramilitary violence. The latest example of this violence was the bomb which last week brutally killed a young British soldier. All over the parish, I found expression of shock at the killing, sympathy for the victim and his relatives, and depression at the endless prolongation of this senseless campaign. The bomb exploded a few yards from the church and right beside the schoolyard wall. It was placed therefore in between two sanctuaries, the sanctuary where God lives and is worshipped by his community, and the sanctuary of the Catholic school, where the children of the community are taught to love God and to follow Jesus Christ's way of love and forgiveness. It was by the mercy of God that no child was killed or seriously injured by the blocks of debris hurled over the wall by the force of the blast. Any passer-by could have been killed. The roof of the Pro-Cathedral was pierced at several places by the fall-out from the blast.

But the worst damage done to the Catholic community by this bomb and by this whole campaign is the spiritual damage of the corruption of consciences by the claim that moral evil is right, that murder is a legitimate political method. The Catholic community is damaged in its deep heart's core by the exposing of children to the sight of the mangled remains of a mutilated body on a sidewalk. I personally witnessed that day the terror in the eyes, the tremor in the voices, the bewilderment in the faces of the children. I personally encountered that day the panic of the mothers. Let those responsible for the horrific experience of those children and those mothers reflect on Our Lord's words about those who scandalise the little ones:

> It would be better for him to be thrown into the sea with a millstone put round his neck than that he should lead astray one of these little ones. (Lk 17:2)

To those who perpetrated that operation and to those who ordered it and who planned it, and to those who direct this whole campaign, I want to say: The people of St Peter's have suffered enough. For their sake, for God's sake, stop this killing. It is not guns and bombs that we need in St Peter's and in West Belfast. It is jobs; it is houses; it is proper school facilities; it is decent amenities for mothers and children and for our old people. Your campaign is only obstructing the struggle for justice for our people. You are piling further misery upon misery for an already much oppressed community.

Preferential Option for the Poor and Mary's Covenant with the Poor

The document published by the Latin American bishops at the close of their meeting in Puebla in 1979 contains a chapter entitled 'A preferential option for the poor'. The words of James Connolly below are quoted from The Workers' Republic, *15 July 1900. The words of Pope St John Paul II are from his message for the World Day of Peace, 1998.*

I quote James Connolly's ringing words:

> Ireland, as distinct from her people, is nothing to me; and the one who is bubbling with love and enthusiasm for 'Ireland' and can yet pass unmoved through our streets and witness all the wrong and the suffering, the shame and degradation, brought upon the people of Ireland – aye, brought by Irish upon Irish– without burning to end it, is, in my opinion a fraud and a liar in his heart, no matter how he loves that combination of chemical elements he is pleased to call 'Ireland'.

It might seem strange for me to be quoting these words in a homily in a Catholic church. But those words of James Connolly are fully in line with the teaching of the Gospels. They are echoed again and again in Catholic social teaching and are closely paralleled in the words of Popes. These words are imbued with the same spirit as that of Pope John Paul II:

> We can no longer tolerate a world in which there live side by side the immensely rich and the miserably poor, the have-nots deprived even of essentials and people who thoughtlessly waste what others so desperately need. … Those living in poverty can wait no longer; they need help now.

Pope John Paul, on one of his visits to Latin America, asked the bishops there to make the Magnificat the basis of their social teaching. Those bishops committed the Church at Medellin in 1968 and again at Puebla to an 'option for the poor'. The Church in Ireland must resolutely make this option for the poor.

Mary, the Mother of Jesus, in her Magnificat, outlines her covenant with God and her 'covenant with the poor'. She pleads before God the rights of the hungry and the needs of the dispossessed of the earth. Not for nothing is Mary called 'Mirror of Justice'.

May her prayers obtain from God for all of us the grace, the motivation and the courage to work, each in his or her own way, for a more just and therefore more peaceful and reconciled society in this country; for, from justice for each comes peace for all.

CONCLUSION

There is a constant theme in the chapters of this book – the sovereignty of God's kingdom of love, peace and justice and the challenge to all Christians in the Ireland of the late twentieth century and early years of the twenty-first century to work and to pray for that kingdom.

Chapter 1 is a poignant reminder of the awful reality and cruel impact of violence in Northern Ireland, particularly on families and communities. The perpetrators of that violence included the IRA and loyalist sectarian killers. The victims of the latter were chosen because of their religion; the targets of the IRA included members of the judiciary and police officers. While always condemning the moral evil of murder and while recognising the devastating effect of murder on the families of victims, Cahal Daly was always hopeful that good would prevail through the building of bridges of understanding, through prayer and through the creation of institutions of justice.

The first part of chapter 2 invites the reader to reflect on the conditions for peace in Northern Ireland – an acceptance of the equal legitimacy of the two traditions of unionism and nationalism and a total commitment to non-violence. The Christian's work for peace must include persevering prayer to the Lord of history to move minds and hearts. The second part of chapter 2 echoes chapter 1 in its reminders of the reach of the callous acts of violence outside Northern Ireland – to London, and to the injustice suffered by the Birmingham Six. There is robustly expressed disappointment at the injustice of the reversal in 1996 by the police of its Garvaghy Road parade decision in the light of loyalist opposition. Again, there is an emphasis on the peaceful pursuit of justice which needs to be intensified in the face of continuing challenges.

The very title of chapter 3 – 'A Civilisation of Love' – captures its main theme. For the Christian, the call to love is universal, extending from the home to creation, to the community and including those of different religious and political beliefs. It is a revolutionary call to a new creation, a new social order infused by prayer and forgiveness.

Chapter 4 focuses on Catholic education, beginning in the home and extending into the faith-based school that is founded on a God-centred vision of life and of truth and which promotes a relationship of love with God in Christ. The crucial role of the teacher standing in the place of Christ as well as *in loco parentis* is highlighted, as is the role of the Catholic school in promoting reconciliation in society.

The imperative of social justice is explored in chapter 5. There is the prospect of 'appalling surprises and shocks' at the Last Judgement for the Christian who has failed to engage effectively with problems such as poverty, unemployment and poor housing or who has dismissed the needy as lazy, scroungers, a burden on society. Mary, who prays the

Magnificat, in which the lowly are raised up, is the model for the response to the cry of the poor.

In his book *Steps on my Pilgrim Journey,* Cardinal Daly stated:

> All the various fields of learning and of literature and of art, of study and of teaching, of language and culture, philosophy and theology, of personal and pastoral experience, to which I have been exposed, have, by God's grace, strengthened my conviction about the truths of our faith and intensified my desire to make that faith known and loved … I take my confidence for the future, Christ's future, from the words from which I took my episcopal motto: 'Jesus Christ is the same today as he was yesterday and as he will be forever' (Heb 13:8).

This book has been inspired by the spirit of that desire of the Cardinal to make the faith known and loved and by his confidence for the future.